✶TAR WARS™
100 OBJECTS

ILLUMINATING ITEMS FROM A GALAXY FAR, FAR AWAY....

STAR WARS
100 OBJECTS

ILLUMINATING ITEMS FROM A GALAXY FAR, FAR AWAY....

WRITTEN BY KRISTIN BAVER

Contents

NEW REPUBLIC ERA

FIRST ORDER ERA

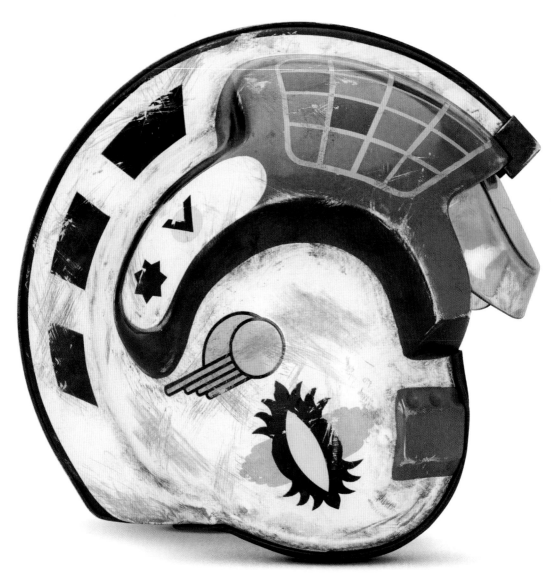

The helmet of John Vander,
leader of Gold Squadron.

Author's Note

I have spent many happy hours in museums around the world, exploring collections of artifacts from our own galaxy that seem to recover people lost to time. From the red-knit sweater worn by TV presenter Fred Rogers in the Smithsonian's National Museum of American History in Washington, D.C., to the legendary Rosetta Stone in London's British Museum, these artifacts transform our understanding of our world and ourselves, connecting us to moments in history. Although the great artists, historical figures, and radical thinkers connected to these archival objects are often long dead, their legacy remains. And through these artifacts, we encounter a portal to commune with the past.

In 2020, when I finished *Skywalker: A Family at War*, an in-world historical biography of the Skywalker family, I bookended the story of three generations with two sacred objects: the mask of Darth Vader and the Skywalker lightsaber. In-universe they are heirlooms for members of the Skywalker dynasty, but in our world these pieces are indelibly linked to the stories we know and love. The mask of Darth Vader conjures the animosity of the Sith, the lost innocence of Anakin, and the Empire's iron fist. The lightsaber, in perfect balance, instead represents light and life, the Jedi Order's proclivity for defending those in need, and the struggle of the practitioners who have been forced to go to war.

I must admit, I was not ready to stop thinking of the Skywalkers as a flesh-and-blood family when my deadline arrived. And after the book was released in April of 2021, rather than return to our reality after months pretending that the legendary Skywalker clan was real, the idea for *Star Wars: 100 Objects* was born.

Within these pages, we have curated a collection of 100 items from each *Star Wars* era seen on screen with the help and patient guidance of the archivists at Skywalker Ranch and the Lucasfilm Archives. Through individual pieces—both historically significant and compelling in their ability to bring to life a culture, a place, or a person—we trace a path through the timeline of the galaxy. We invite you to let these items tell their own stories. Together, these artifacts and heirlooms—from the Great Sith Wars Bas-Relief to Rey Skywalker's lightsaber—combine like threads in the tapestry of significant events and figures at the center of the *Star Wars* saga.

Kristin Baver

Republic Era

For more than 1,000 years, the Galactic Republic
unites star systems in a democracy clustered around the
Core World of Coruscant. The great Jedi Knights,
mysterious robe-clad individuals devoted to the mystical
energy of the Force, serve as peacekeepers and guardians
of justice. It is a time of harmony, after the Sith have been
vanquished by the defenders of the light.

But there is a ripple of darkness, a tremble beneath the
thrum of prosperity and egalitarianism—a disturbance in
the Force itself. At the heart of the disruption: a young
Force-sensitive boy named Anakin Skywalker, discovered
on Tatooine and believed by some to be the Chosen One
of prophecy.

Instead, darkness rises. The creation of the Grand
Army of the Republic and the ensuing three years of
turmoil across the galaxy will bring the Galactic Republic
to its knees.

1

Great Sith Wars Bas-Relief

Location: Coruscant
Date: c. 4,000 BBY

Across the millennia, the forces of light and darkness have been locked in a cycle that has tipped the balance of the Force time and again. In ancient times, a Jedi schism ushered in a new sect of believers who worshipped the dark alone: the Sith.

This faction challenged the Jedi and their supporters on the battlefield in a sprawling conflict known as the Great Sith Wars. They raged for centuries before the reformation of the Republic—the period of unity that would evolve

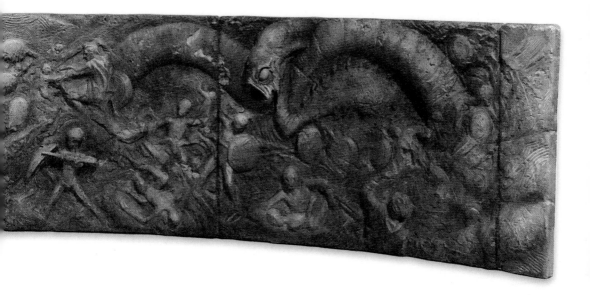

into the High Republic. Those years of unrest gave rise to some remarkable artifacts, such as this spectacular frieze, which once hung in Supreme Chancellor Sheev Palpatine's office in the Galactic Senate on Coruscant. During his tumultuous years in office, Jedi and members of the Galactic Senate alike were ushered past the frieze en route to clandestine meetings with high-ranking officials. Palpatine's fascination with ancient history and the arts was clear from his collection of artifacts, yet the bas-relief stands out for its symbolic significance. At the outbreak of the Clone Wars, it was not long before Palpatine revealed his true allegiance by declaring that the Jedi were enemies of the Republic and must be annihilated.

Highly prized by Palpatine, the frieze was allegedly discovered during an archaeological dig on an unknown planet. Treasure hunters and unscrupulous collectors like Palpatine purchased unique and priceless artifacts such as this on the black market.

Similar bas-reliefs have been found at the excavation sites of Sith and Jedi temples. They probably once decorated circular chambers surrounding altars.

In four full panels and two half panels, this high-relief carving tells the story of an ancient battle. The individuals depicted on the relief are not soldiers in the usual sense. They are seemingly Force-wielders, armed with lightsabers and forever locked in combat with the grotesque, hollow-eyed minions of darkness.

A trio of warriors can be seen preparing for battle, with a seemingly female fighter at right carrying what appears to be a lightsaber. Without pigment to determine the color of her blade, we cannot know for sure if she fights for the light or the dark.

It is hard to determine which side is winning. A robed figure on the first panel may be emerging victorious to one viewer, while another sees the same figure being enveloped by the horde in a decisive defeat.

An apparently female warrior to the right stands at the ready holding what appears to be a lightsaber, the weapon of the Jedi. However, we know that a corrupted version of the saber was favored by the Sith, only distinguished by the color of its blade.

If pigment once helped to clarify this portion of the story, it has been lost to the ages, worn away by time and the elements. Elsewhere on the frieze, other robed Jedi join the fray, with one seeming to sit astride a beast of burden. This warrior appears to be riding the creature into battle against a serpentine creature angled toward the viewer, its hungry maw agape.

A Sith-aligned minion prepares to fire an ancient, lightbow-like weapon.

A mythical beast, similar in appearance to a dewback, enters the fray carrying a robed rider.

The Great Sith Wars Bas-Relief is an especially important artifact in the history of the galaxy. It is both an early example of visual storytelling and a window into the conflict between the Jedi and the Sith—the ever-present struggle between the light and the dark. The relic's prominent place in the halls of governance just before the Republic yielded to the encroaching Sith darkness makes it a potent reminder that the eternal battle of good against evil is never truly won.

A bug-eyed serpent crashes into view as the fight plays out below.

2

Japor Snippet Pendant

Location: Tatooine
Date: 32 BBY

This simple carved pendant may be almost worthless as an item of jewelry, but it is a priceless artifact when exploring the impact three generations of the Skywalker family had on shaping galactic events.

Made from a discarded chunk of japor, one of the woody plants tough enough to survive on Tatooine, it was carved by Anakin Skywalker before he joined the Jedi Order. The young slave may have stolen the pendant's raw materials from Watto's workshop, where he was forced to work.

Worn smooth by time, the details of the carving show natural elements coalescing at the design's center. Anakin was a naturally powerful conduit for the energy of the Force, but it is unlikely that these simple shapes had any symbolic meaning for him at the time.

Anakin gave the snippet to Padmé Amidala when she was in her first term as Queen of Naboo, just before he embarked on an exciting future as a Jedi Knight. It was a gesture of gratitude, but also something more: Anakin was smitten with Padmé, who had befriended him while posing as a servant, and feared that he would never see her again. Anakin was determined to give her something to remember him by—hence this pendant, made with care by his own hands especially for the woman that, unbeknownst to him, he would one day marry.

Despite Padmé's royal status, Anakin's touchingly simple japor snippet became one of her most treasured possessions. At the time of her tragically young death, she was carried to her crypt with the token clutched between her lifeless hands. For some years afterward, the snippet was enshrined near the entrance of her tomb.

3

Cordé's Robe

Location: Naboo
Date: 22 BBY

Amid the sumptuous fabrics and fine garments in Padmé Amidala's personal collection, this soot-blackened travel robe stands out, both for its appearance and the story of sacrifice it evokes.

Bell sleeves and black-beaded accents elevate this originally plain white travel robe, sewn from a thick brocade fabric with a distinctive crosshatch pattern embellished in the weave. The subtle detail and palette were something of a fashion statement reflecting Senator Amidala's stance on the impending galactic conflict. The gown's snowy hue echoed Amidala's hope that peace and democracy would endure throughout the galaxy.

This robe was last worn by Amidala's decoy, Cordé, during Amidala's return to the Galactic Senate ahead of the critical vote on the creation of the Grand Army of the Republic. Amidala's penchant for using decoys dated from the earliest days of her reign as queen. Elaborate headpieces, makeup, and an array of robes and gowns allowed the real Amidala to trade places with her nearly identical handmaidens. This enabled her to embark on dangerous missions in secret or, as in this case, to protect her own life when it became clear she had become a Separatist target.

Sadly, a bomb aboard Amidala's ship sent Cordé and six other loyal security guards to their deaths. With her dying words, Cordé apologized for failing Amidala, who, disguised in the fatigues of a Naboo pilot, had rushed to Cordé's side with no concern for her own safety.

During the queen's reign, the handmaidens of Amidala sat among high-ranking dignitaries all but unnoticed. They deliberately blended into the background, watching, listening, and collecting information for their mistress, whom they held in the utmost esteem. They shielded her identity when called upon to act in her stead, and were prepared to lay down their lives to protect her. Cordé's brave sacrifice, symbolized by this tattered, scorched robe, is a stark reminder of the life-and-death nature of a handmaiden's position in Naboo society.

4

Bust of Count Dooku

Location: Coruscant
Date: c. 42 BBY

The Lost. The name suggests a precious few, adrift and astray. Within the ranks of the Jedi Order, the Lost were a group of individuals whose paths diverged from the teachings of the Force. They had all become disillusioned in some way, but perhaps none more so than Count Dooku of Serenno.

This heavy bronzium bust exudes extraordinary presence, the eyes hollowed with an unseeing, but still unsettling, gaze. Lines etched in the cheeks and forehead betray a life of struggle and worry.

Dooku was abandoned in his youth by his noble father, who was terrified by his child's Force-sensitivity. He trained as the Padawan of Jedi Master Yoda—who rarely took on pupils—and attained the rank of Jedi Master, along with one of the 12 seats on the Jedi High Council. An expert swordsman who trained young Jedi in the art of lightsaber dueling, Dooku also took on his own Padawans, including the Jedi Qui-Gon Jinn.

His tutelage by some of the most notable Jedi of the time and exemplary record of service stands in stark contrast to Dooku's eventual fate. Disillusioned by the corruption he saw festering in the Republic and by the Jedi Order's close links with officialdom, Dooku left the Order to reclaim his place as Count of Serenno. But more than just cutting ties with the Order, Dooku became aligned with the Sith and the Separatist movement, commanding a droid army that fought at the Battle of Geonosis and on countless battlefields during the three-year Clone Wars.

After his departure from the Order, the bust stood in the halls of the Jedi Archive on Coruscant. Its face embodies strength and humility, the finest qualities upheld by the Jedi in their prime. Yet in those hollow eyes, darkness lingers. And Dooku's sad fate—killed with his own lightsaber by Anakin Skywalker—is a reminder that anyone, no matter how potentially heroic and noble, can be seduced by the dark side.

5

Shmi's Aeromagnifier

Location: Tatooine
Date: 32 BBY

Shmi Skywalker is best known as the matriarch of the Skywalker family, whose members, over the course of three generations, played crucial roles in galactic history. In another life, Shmi's place in the tapestry of the greater galaxy might have put her on a throne. But life can be cruel, and, for many years, Shmi's lot was servitude and slavery.

Shmi was an exceptional mother who doted on her son, Anakin, and filled his early years with love. During the time Shmi and Anakin lived as slaves to the junk boss Watto, Shmi made their meager hovel into a home and did everything she could to provide her son with a moral center in his life.

Shmi also helped Anakin to develop his mechanical ingenuity, and in fact passed on some of the skills that gave young Ani the knowledge to build his own protocol droid from scrap. At a workstation inside the Skywalker abode, Shmi spent long hours earning extra wupiupi by cleaning computer memory devices, aided by an aeromagnifier like this one. The device was a rare gesture of kindness from Watto, gifted to Shmi in a show of benevolence toward a hardworking slave who gave so much of her life to support his.

The Skywalker home was feebly lit at night, but the aeromagnifier's illuminator rings and magnifying lens allowed Shmi to toil long after Tatooine's twin suns had set and her eyes had become fatigued. Held aloft by a repulsor hood, the device would have filled the Skywalker abode with its soothing thrum late into the night as Anakin slept nearby.

6

Kaminoan Saberdart

Origin: Kamino
Date: 22 BBY

The people of Kamino were often lauded for their scientific achievements in the field of cloning—creating millions of identical human soldiers in the lead-up to the Clone Wars. However, those who are most interested in the creation of life often show an equal fascination with its opposite. So it was not surprising that the same great minds who created the Grand Army of the Republic also conceived this small and deadly weapon.

In the crowded and chaotic lower levels of Coruscant, a saberdart was a common weapon of choice for assassins. Fired from a KiSteer 1284 projectile rifle, the dart's barbed, winglike features made it extremely difficult to remove once it was firmly dug into flesh. The bounty hunter Jango Fett used a saberdart to kill the assassin Zam Wesell. Fett fired the toxic projectile—the poison was stored in a chamber in the dart's barrel—from a safe distance and struck Wesell in the throat. She was just about to tell the Jedi Anakin Skywalker and Obi-Wan Kenobi that Fett had hired her to assassinate the Naboo Senator Padmé Amidala, but died almost instantly.

Small incisions along the dart's base were the only clues to its planet of origin. The one that killed Zam Wesell was identified by Dexter "Dex" Jettster, the well-traveled owner of Dex's Diner, as coming from the planet Kamino. Without Dex's help, it would have been almost impossible for the Jedi to trace, because at that time Kamino was scrubbed from galaxy maps and databases to conceal the Republic's creation of its clone army. Ironically, the DNA template for that army belonged to none other than saberdart specialist Jango Fett himself.

7

Sith Lightsabers

Location: Various
Date: c. 32 BBY

At first glance, one might mistake this hilt as the weapon of a Jedi. Look closely, however, and you will find a perversion of the light. This saber hides a corrupted kyber crystal made to bleed a sickly red.

Where the lightsabers of the Jedi were principally employed for defense, the nearly identical weapons of the Sith were made for destruction. This saberstaff, with its deadly dual blades, is a prime example of the devastation that could be wrought in the hands of pure evil.

Each Force-wielder who has built a lightsaber has constructed a unique artifact created to fit their personal aesthetic and fighting style. In some cases their lightsaber might pay homage to their species and ancestry. To the vast majority of beings across the galaxy who lacked Force-sensitivity, these laser swords, whether belonging to Jedi or Sith, could appear interchangeable.

In countless stories, the Sith and their followers were initially mistaken for keepers of the peace. As soon as people saw their blades blaze crimson, however, it was all too obvious that the Sith's interests and intentions were totally opposed to those of the Jedi Knights.

Before Darth Vader and Count Dooku served Darth Sidious, another villain kneeled at his feet: Darth Maul. A Zabrak Nightbrother from the mists of Dathomir, Maul's horn-headed visage was a fearsome sight. Yet his real power came from his preternatural agility and his skill with his double-bladed lightsaber.

On the besieged world of Naboo, Maul used this formidable weapon to murder the Jedi Qui-Gon Jinn before he, in turn, was felled by Jinn's apprentice, Obi-Wan Kenobi. The duel ended when both Maul and his lightsaber were cleaved in two. The Sith Lord was widely believed to be dead, although his enemies subsequently learned that he had somehow survived, fueled by his burning desire for vengeance.

And what of his weapon? Although a Sith no longer after this crushing defeat, Maul reinvented himself several times over the ensuing years. Ultimately, he became one of the most powerful crime lords in the galactic underworld. This double-bladed lightsaber relates to a period in his youth when he served the Sith's cause. For a brief time, Maul changed the course of history by killing the Jedi Knight who discovered—and would have trained—Anakin Skywalker.

After Maul's presumed demise, Darth Sidious took a new pupil in Darth Tyranus. Earlier in life Tyranus was a ruler of Serenno known as the Jedi Master Dooku.

Dooku's lightsaber had an elegantly curved hilt fashioned to complement his fighting style. Its grip is similar to that of a dueling blaster. He was known among those who sparred with him at the Jedi Temple as an especially skilled and agile opponent. Dooku's superb dueling technique was comprised of precision moves, formal lunges, and ripostes, hardwired during his days training at the Jedi Temple.

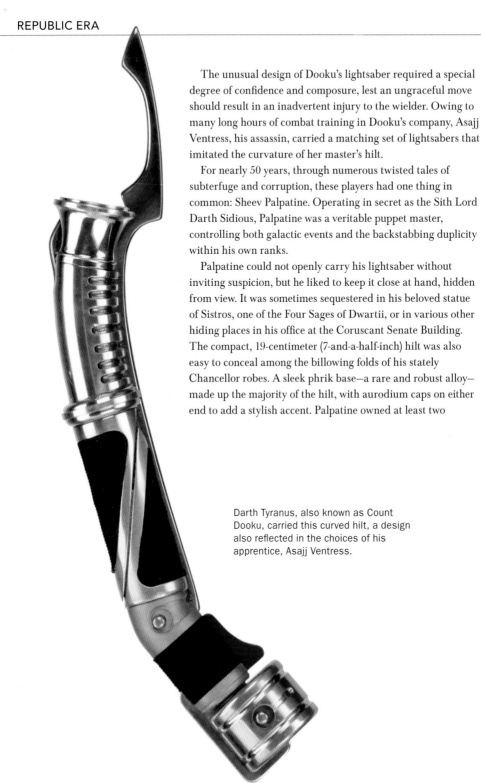

The unusual design of Dooku's lightsaber required a special degree of confidence and composure, lest an ungraceful move should result in an inadvertent injury to the wielder. Owing to many long hours of combat training in Dooku's company, Asajj Ventress, his assassin, carried a matching set of lightsabers that imitated the curvature of her master's hilt.

For nearly 50 years, through numerous twisted tales of subterfuge and corruption, these players had one thing in common: Sheev Palpatine. Operating in secret as the Sith Lord Darth Sidious, Palpatine was a veritable puppet master, controlling both galactic events and the backstabbing duplicity within his own ranks.

Palpatine could not openly carry his lightsaber without inviting suspicion, but he liked to keep it close at hand, hidden from view. It was sometimes sequestered in his beloved statue of Sistros, one of the Four Sages of Dwartii, or in various other hiding places in his office at the Coruscant Senate Building. The compact, 19-centimeter (7-and-a-half-inch) hilt was also easy to conceal among the billowing folds of his stately Chancellor robes. A sleek phrik base—a rare and robust alloy—made up the majority of the hilt, with aurodium caps on either end to add a stylish accent. Palpatine owned at least two

Darth Tyranus, also known as Count Dooku, carried this curved hilt, a design also reflected in the choices of his apprentice, Asajj Ventress.

identical blades, and was skilled at fighting with two sabers in combat against multiple assailants.

It is a common refrain that only two Sith can operate at any given time—a master and an apprentice. This is due to the ruthlessness that is the very essence of the Sith's philosophy. Once Sith apprentices become powerful enough, they invariably overpower their teachers, murdering their masters and taking their place. They then school a pupil of their own and the cycle begins again.

To become a Sith is to be inherently distrustful, conniving, and cruel. There is plenty of evidence that students and masters alike flouted the ritualistic "Rule of Two," whether out of vengeance, ambition, or fear.

The lightsabers of the Sith, and the villainous creatures who employed them, are no longer a threat to the light. But these artifacts serve as a warning that the darkness is not easily dissuaded from its purpose: to snuff out all that is good in the galaxy. And morbid vengeance can be as potent as idealism in fueling a cause.

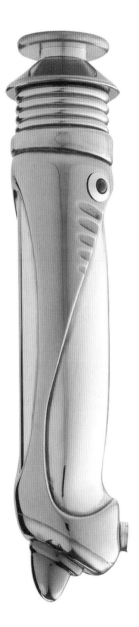

Palpatine liked to keep his compact lightsaber with its vibrant red blade nearby or on his person, but he rarely resorted to it. If trouble threatened, he preferred to project bolts of lightning from his fingertips, wounding opponents from a safe distance.

8

Wookiee Clarion

Location: Kashyyyk
Date: 300 BBY–19 BBY

The towering Wookiee natives of Kashyyyk were intimidating in stature and strength. However, unless antagonized, these giants were genuinely gentle. They were also renowned for their empathetic nature and a refined artistic skill that paid homage to their beloved homeworld. This clarion was handmade on Kashyyyk in a laborious process that merged natural wood from the wroshyr tree, hand-hammered bronzium plating, and natural cerulean gemstones.

In times of prosperity and peace a call from a clarion brought a clan together for friendly gatherings, meetings, and festivities, including the Wookiee celebration of family, joy, and harmony known as Life Day. In times of war, the horn played an even more vital role, sounding the alarm to unite scattered tribes against a common enemy.

Although the origin of this particular horn is unknown, a similar instrument was utilized in the final days of the Clone Wars, as the Wookiees of Kashyyyk were besieged by a Separatist attack.

The horn was crafted to wrap around the Wookiee player, cradling their torso and making the instrument comfortable to wear on the move. Thanks to a Wookiee's remarkable lung strength, the horn's sonorous bellow carried for more than 20 kilometers (12 miles). The artisan who made the clarion took great pains to adorn the instrument with hammered decorations, a clear indicator that it was used in sacred rituals over many years, and was an heirloom celebrating the identity of the tribe.

The various swirling decorations on the horn are believed to be the insignia of the Porr'trrr tribe. This clarion has a brass plate, affixed among several keys used to change the pitch of the sound, on which a portrait of a noble Wookiee looks back toward the player. The individual depicted in the etching may be the maker's self-portrait, a way to mark their work. Alternatively, it could be the image of a tribe elder, someone of importance to the horn's owner, or the face of the horn's owner and player.

Metal panel showing
Wookiee portrait engraving.

9

Sages of Dwartii Statues

Date: Displayed c. 19 BBY
Location: Coruscant

The Four Sages of Dwartii are said to have hailed from the Inner Rim world of the same name. It is unclear if these statues—cast centuries ago—were created on their homeworld or elsewhere, as the Sages' philosophical views and legendary status traveled throughout the galaxy.

Head bowed, hands clasped as if in prayer, the statue representing the ancient philosopher Sistros Nevet is an especially revealing relic of the Republic. It serves as a warning—sadly unheeded—of the Imperial regime that would soon replace the longstanding democratic union of planets.

This neuranium statue with its gleaming bronzium finish—a sinister monument to an arcane and ancient past—stood in the office of Supreme Chancellor Sheev Palpatine. It was later displayed in his throne room after he became ruler of the Galactic Empire.

During Palpatine's days as Supreme Chancellor, a much smaller version of Sistros's statue was perched atop the speaker staff carried by Mas Amedda, the Chagrian vice chair of the Galactic Senate during the Clone Wars. Amedda was one of Palpatine's chief advisors, and remained faithful to him throughout his rule as Emperor.

In life, Sistros was a Nouanese minister and lawmaker who was known to be an emotionless ruler. Cold and calculating, she was often accused of using her position during the formation of the original Galactic Republic for selfish ends. It is little wonder that the unscrupulous Palpatine, the man who would become Emperor, idolized this particular sage.

The statue of Sistros was, in effect, a testament to Palpatine's own bid for unlimited power and his secret devotion to the Sith. It remained one of his most treasured possessions after he became Emperor. The enigmatic artifact looked on as he held court in the new Imperial Palace, controversially erected inside the battle-scarred shell that had once been the Jedi Temple.

A small, hollow chamber in the statue, seemingly dating from the time the piece was cast, was used by Palpatine to conceal his greatest secret: the red-bladed lightsaber of his alter ego, Darth Sidious. This weapon clearly marked him out as a Sith occultist. That Palpatine should choose to hide this clue to his true intentions in the statue of Sistros is ironic—perhaps deliberately so—given that the philosopher is represented as a cloaked figure, shrouded in mystery.

Just like Palpatine, Sistros did not act alone. Her statue is part of a set that also comprises the sages Faya Rodemos, Yanjon Zelmar, and Braata Danlos. Little is known about the other members of this quartet as they lived in the Inner Rim a thousand years before the Galactic Empire came to power. As philosophers, they influenced the politics of their day, including the laws that governed the Republic. They were doubtless controversial lawmakers with contentious views, but the Republic nevertheless thrived for centuries as a bastion of democracy.

Unlike Sistros's elegant and mysterious depiction—like a goddess wrapped in fine cloaks with a hood to conceal her features—the other three sages are represented more clearly. The statue of Faya Rodemos, which used to stand like a sentry by Palpatine's office door, wears a mask that obscures the mouth, as if silencing the sage. Arms crossed in supplication or perhaps bound by an assailant, it looks as if Faya is being restrained.

Yanjon Zelmar is depicted wearing a regal headdress and reaching inside one sleeve, as if seeking to locate some treasure or seize a weapon.

Lastly, the statue of Braata Danlos appears to be wearing a helmet and holding a staff or swordlike weapon, as if preparing to go to war.

Frozen in time, the four statues of the Sages of Dwartii radiate a mysterious power. The precise nature of that power it is up to the viewer to decide upon.

Left to right: Faya Rodemos, Yanjon Zelmar, and Braata Danlos.

10

Podracer

Location: Tatooine
Date: 32 BBY

Every podracer is a unique—and uniquely dangerous—machine, a minuscule cockpit leashed to two powerful engines hurtling around a racecourse at perilous speeds. Operating such a contraption takes great skill, concentration, and superhuman reflexes. Even watching a podrace is not advisable for those of a nervous disposition.

A favorite sport among gamblers and swindlers throughout galactic history, podracing appeals to risk-takers of all kinds. Those wishing to make a few extra credits at the podracing track by wagering on the spectacle can sit at a safe distance and watch their best guess turn to triumph or fiery defeat. Anyone with the requisite skills can procure or cobble together a podracer and enter the race each Boonta Eve. Others wishing to get close to the action without the inherent risks may choose to assist the podracers as crew.

Breakdowns and spectacular burnouts are a big part of the fun for the crowd. A small mechanical malfunction in these rickety, overpowered vehicles can leave a racer sputtering at the starting line or—if it occurs during the race—result in a fiery demise.

Many of those who enter the arena are killed or maimed in their reckless quest for glory. Those who survive are often left riding on little more than debris by the time the winner is declared. Few podracer vehicles remain intact after a race.

In the year 32 BBY, a nine-year-old human slave named Anakin Skywalker won the Boonta Eve Classic in this pod, a customized Radon-Ulzer craft. Built by Anakin in secret, this distinctive silver-and-blue podracer measures about 3.15 meters (10 feet 4 inches) long. Smaller and more aerodynamic than many competitors' vehicles, it was able to reach speeds of more than 1,000 kph (620 mph).

Even at such a young age Anakin was a brilliant mechanic, so it is little wonder that he designed a podracer capable of achieving the extreme speeds needed to win. It certainly did not hurt that at the helm was a future Jedi Knight, whose nascent abilities with the Force surely contributed to his incredible reflexes that day.

Anakin faced plenty of tough competition at the Mos Espa Grand Arena. Among the 18 entrants were several notable podracers, including Ark Roose, Ratts Tyerell, Ben Quadinaros, Gasgano, and Dud Bolt.

In the high-stakes world of podracing, cheating is officially frowned upon, yet validated time and again with fame and fortune. Among those most notorious for their penchant for sabotage and bending race rules was a male Dug named Sebulba. Anakin's main rival in the Boonta Eve Classic, his chariot was an orange repulsorcraft. Although its twin engines were destroyed during that race, the cockpit remains, a trophy of defeat. Sebulba was a particularly unscrupulous contender, with a long history of wins that kept his coffers full and earned him esteem among those who cared not how he won, but only that his streak continued. Cheating alone could not have scored Sebulba so many victories—he also possessed great natural talent for

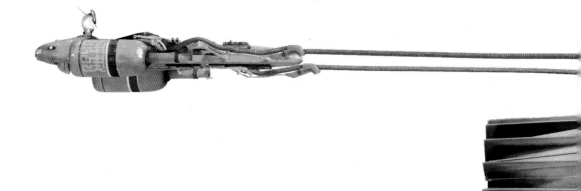

The longstanding Mos Espa podracing champion Sebulba operated this craft. His small pod was powered along by illegally overclocked hulking engines.

the sport. Nevertheless, the hidden flamethrower, ion disrupters, and magna-spikes tucked away in his podracer, as well as its split-X engines reinforced to double as ramming devices, certainly helped to increase his chances of winning.

Sebulba's tactics were at best unfair and at worst illegal, but with the criminal Hutt Clan running the podracing circuit, there was no authority prepared to challenge the Dug's methods. Integrity aside, Sebulba's record of wins was impressive, until the fateful day when a human boy, Anakin Skywalker, defeated him.

11

Plo Koon's Antiox Mask

Location: Dorin
Date: 45 BBY

On the world of Dorin, the native clans of the Kel Dor people thrive in an environment uniquely suited to their evolved anatomy. Instead of the oxygen-rich atmosphere of worlds hospitable to the human species, Dorin is covered in predominantly helium-based gases, to which the planet's flora and fauna are perfectly adapted.

The oxygen mix that sustains many species on Core Worlds like Coruscant is deadly to the Kel Dors without technological intervention. For those restless few eager to explore the galaxy, the Kel Dors developed protective goggles to shield their sensitive eyes and an antiox mask to provide life support. This rebreather, which once belonged to the Jedi Master Plo Koon, filters out harmful oxygen. Attached to his face with a seal, it was connected to the extrasensory organs on either side of his head. A filtration vent was situated directly over his nostril flaps. At the bottom of the metal mask, two points resembling long fangs housed what are thought to be the most sensitive parts of a Kel Dor's anatomy. The detail along the nose ridge, chin, and jowls is purely for decoration.

Master Plo's antiox mask made his facial expressions unreadable, but he was regarded as a calming presence with an even temper and a booming voice—undoubtedly amplified by his rebreather. Sadly, Master Plo was killed in the line of duty over Cato Neimoidia during the last days of the Clone Wars.

Master Plo's antiox mask is etched with a pattern unique to his clan. Although, like other Jedi, he was placed with the Order early in life and its members became his new family unit, Master Plo proudly retained his mask as a lasting link to the house of his birth and to his homeworld.

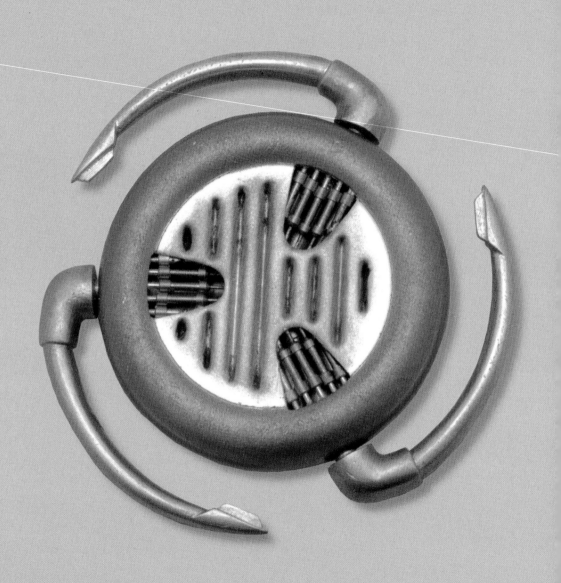

12

Imagecaster Holoprojector

Location: Coruscant
Date: c. 30 BBY

In a galaxy so vast, Imagecaster holoprojectors were an essential communication tool for wealthy wanderers and those carrying information, mementos, and personal messages. The compact, disc-like base displays a simple image, records audio, or, with a reliable uplink to a larger comm network, projects a grainy hologram to someone light years away. The three tines attached to the disc can be folded down to make the Imagecaster into a small, free-standing pedestal.

Holoprojector technology has since become much more sophisticated. The holo-feed now allows messages to be displayed so clearly it almost seems as if the person on the other end were in the room, larger than life. At the time this example was in use, credits were not funneled into perfecting reception or boosting the prevailing blue tinge of images. Holoprojectors were most commonly used by government officials and military strategists. As long as a message could be received clearly, the orders followed, and the battle won, image quality was of little or no interest to them.

This particular Imagecaster was last used preloaded with a simple holo-message that showed a J-type 327 Nubian starship—the same make and model used by the Royal House of Naboo during the time of the Trade Federation's blockade of the planet. The disc was probably part of the Republic-era ship's basic equipment, an aid to the procurement of parts and services should the vessel require repairs while far from home.

Many years later, Obi-Wan Kenobi employed an Imagecaster to contact Leia's adoptive father, Bail Organa, during the Jedi's mission to rescue the kidnapped young princess.

13

Padmé Amidala's Wedding Veil

Location: Naboo
Date: c. 22 BBY

This piece from Padmé Amidala's personal wardrobe has an especially intriguing story attached to it. As war broke out on Geonosis, signaling the beginning of the Republic's downfall, Padmé retreated to her homeworld Naboo's beautiful Lake Country. The young senator wore this beaded veil at her secret wedding to the Jedi Anakin Skywalker. Their marriage was either filed under pseudonyms, redacted from official archives, or simply never recorded. Otherwise Anakin would almost certainly have been ejected from the Jedi Order for marrying.

The origin of the veil itself is unknown. The fine white lace traditionally symbolizes purity, while the elaborate beading indicates that the headpiece was embellished by experienced, trusted hands who intended it to last a long time. Indeed, the veil may have been passed down as a family heirloom from generation to generation.

As Padmé rose in political prominence, her handmaidens became known for reinforcing her clothing to ward off attackers, but this accessory lacks any discernible armored components. Given that the ceremony itself was attended only by Anakin, a Naboo holy man, and a pair of trusted droids—R2-D2 and C-3PO—it is clear that Amidala saw no need for protection at this moment of celebration.

The secret location, the few individuals present, and the sensitivity of the ceremony provided all the shielding needed. With no royal subjects looking on, no Galactic Senate to address, and no enemies to broker negotiations with, on this special day Padmé felt free to shed formal makeup, and pomp and ceremony. Looking upon this pretty veil, it is easy to imagine her happiness. Perhaps for the first time since being crowned Queen of Naboo, Padmé was simply able to be herself.

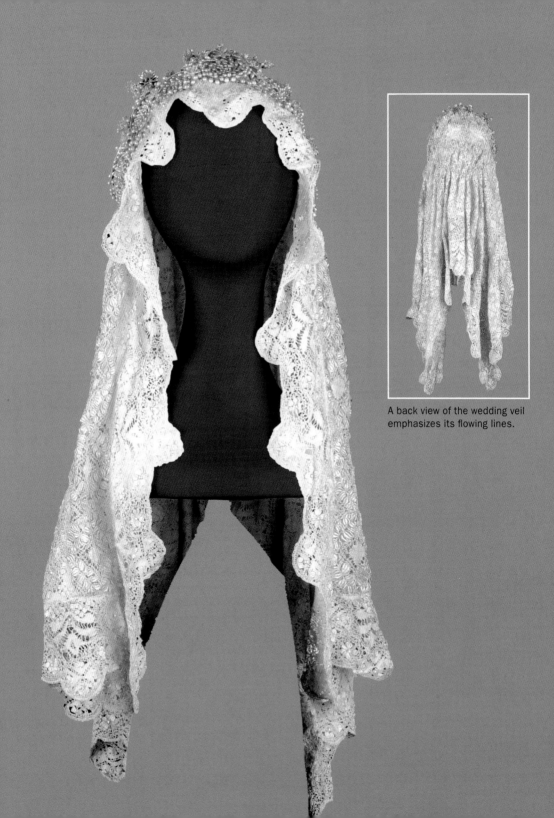

A back view of the wedding veil
emphasizes its flowing lines.

14

Watto's Chance Cube

Location: Tatooine
Date: c. 32 BBY

Games of chance are played throughout the galaxy, but this little cube altered the course of galactic history.

The Toydarian junk dealer Watto was not known for being fair or scrupulous in business among the denizens of Mos Espa. For a time, he owned Shmi Skywalker and her young son Anakin, a small family he won in a bet with Gardulla the Hutt. Ironically, Watto's love of gambling would also lose him his claim over Anakin's life.

On this cube, three faces are marked red while the other three are colored blue. Thrown by many hands over the years, the paint has faded and the edges have worn smooth. The dirt and dust of the arid world of Tatooine, mixed with grime from players' unwashed palms, have become part of the cube's patina.

Before the Boonta Eve Podrace of 32 BBY, the Jedi Qui-Gon Jinn entered Anakin into the competition with the agreement that, if he won, Watto would provide Qui-Gon with parts to repair his starship. To increase the wager, Qui-Gon used his ship as collateral in a secondary bet for Anakin's freedom. Watto was notorious for entering young Anakin into podrace competitions and then betting against him, aware that the dangerous sport typically did not favor the relatively slow reflexes of a human pilot. Watto also knew that the Dug contender Sebulba was especially skilled at cheating. He accepted the bet, confident that Anakin would lose, and also because he had probably weighted his chance cube in his favor. It is also possible that Qui-Gon used the Force to turn the chance cube from red to blue—the outcome he wanted.

Thanks to Anakin's developing Force-sensitive reflexes and the luck that sometimes attends the brave, he did win. Anakin was not only freed from slavery but able to leave Tatooine to pursue his destiny as a Jedi Padawan.

15

A99 Aquata Breather

Location: Coruscant
Date in use: 400–19 BBY

Although the A99 Aquata breather was employed by the Jedi in the later years of the Galactic Republic, it evokes the Order's earlier age of exploration in the days of the High Republic, when reliable hyperspace travel began to connect planets across the galaxy like never before. In place of their ceremonial white robes, the Jedi of the time commonly wore rugged brown leather garments for missions to new worlds and lawless, far-flung territories.

Despite their ability to harness the Force, Jedi explorers often encountered inhospitable worlds and ecosystems where survival was impossible without the aid of technology. For instance, on the world of Naboo, where the Gungans dwelled in watery Otoh Gunga, Jedi diplomats used devices such as these to deliver their hopes for peace in person.

The A99 was a highly specialized tool that spoke to a Jedi's commitment to endure danger and discomfort on their quest for knowledge and a deeper understanding of the galaxy. It was essential for crossing large bodies of water without the protection of a pod or other vehicle. Hinges on either side allowed this small underwater breathing apparatus to be folded into a single linear module for convenient storage. Small filtration mechanisms on either side of the intake regulator processed oxygen from environments without breathable atmospheres. These deceptively simple filters could pull breathable gases from both smoke and water.

Each Jedi explorer possessed a variety of tools to enable them to adapt to whatever environmental conditions they encountered. A comlink allowed the Jedi and other travelers to comunicate with each other. Jedi explorers also used small holoprojectors to record vital data or transmit urgent messages when audio alone was not sufficient.

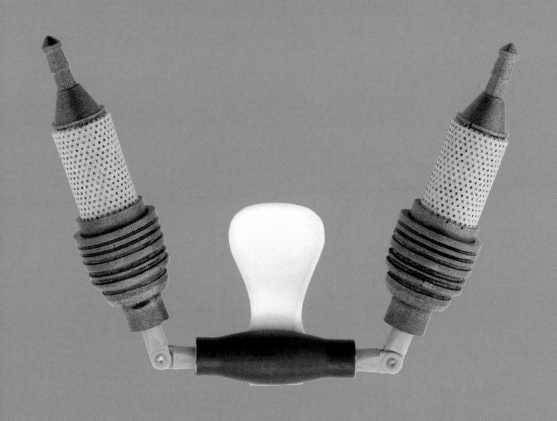

16

Neimoidian Mechno-Chair

Location: Cato Neimoidia
Date: 32 BBY

This thronelike mechno-chair once carried its owner on four skittering, robotic legs. A relic from a dignitary's palace on the affluent colony world of Cato Neimoidia, the chair represents the oppressive wealth of the barons of the Trade Federation.

Much of the chair is exquisitely carved from wood, forming the cradle-like base. On either side, spherical medallions etched with a sun motif stretch upward. When viewed from the front, the back of the chair suggests two wings. From the side, the overall design appears to be something more akin to a beast's fangs or sharp horns, the curvature ending in a fine and potentially lethal point. The padded seat is upholstered in animal hide, both an indication to peers of the owner's wealth and their dominance over the unsuspecting creature that was skinned for this purpose. Only the legs, which were controlled by a small datapad concealed in the armrest, relied on technology for functionality.

Each mechno-chair was painstakingly created by Neimoidian artisans, a time-consuming process that added to the manufacturing cost. Wealthy Neimoidians who could afford such excess furnished their homes with similar items and also traveled with their mechno-chairs off-world. These robotic, mobile thrones immediately conveyed a sense of superiority and prosperity. Trade Federation Viceroy Nute Gunray took a chair similar to this one on his ill-fated trip to the city of Theed during the trade dispute of 32 BBY.

Now a relic of the period, mechno-chairs are a symbol of bygone grandeur, a pre-Clone Wars affectation from an amoral society that prized wealth above all else. Darth Sidious kept one as a trophy of his successful exploitation of the Trade Federation, which played a key role in his schemes. The curator of the Imperial Museum also moved about using a mechno-chair.

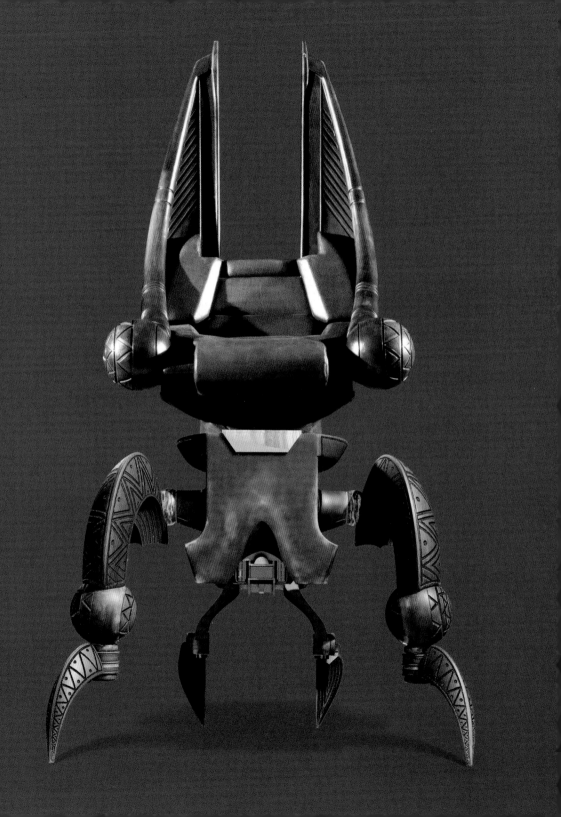

17

Queen Amidala's Senatorial Gown

Location: Naboo
Date: 32 BBY

Elected to the throne of Naboo at just 14 years of age, Padmé Amidala, born to the house of Naberrie, was her planet's sovereign for two terms. She then continued her public service in the Galactic Senate.

As monarch, Queen Amidala presented herself as the living symbol of Naboo. She wore the striking traditional makeup adopted by all the planet's queens. This consisted of a white pallor with red accents and, in accordance with ancient custom, the scar of remembrance. This symbol of Naboo's past suffering marked her lower lip.

Amidala's ceremonial gowns spoke to the luxury, history, and duty of the crown. Her wardrobe contained many garments worthy of appreciation and display, crafted with the utmost care from the finest materials. Yet it is her senatorial gown that stands alone as emblematic of her unwavering compassion for her people and of her resolve to speak out on their behalf. For it was only within the Galactic Senate that Amidala had the opportunity to wield real power to effect change by influencing new legislation and the decrees of the Supreme Chancellor.

In the year 32 BBY, Amidala chose to wear this gown to make an impassioned plea to free her planet from the invading forces of the Trade Federation. In so doing, she openly challenged Supreme Chancellor Finis Valorum in the cavernous Senate rotunda. Amidala demanded immediate aid to wrest Naboo from the tyrannical traders blockading her home.

The veracity of her accusations was challenged that day by the delegate from the Trade Federation. Perhaps as a ploy to delay taking any action, Valorum asked Amidala to defer her motion and leave the matter to the legal system to decide. She replied: "I will not defer. I have come before you to resolve this attack on our sovereignty now. I was not elected to watch my people suffer and die while you discuss this invasion in a committee."

Amidala then proceeded to denounce Valorum and—following the advice

of the manipulative Naboo Senator Palpatine—move for a Vote of No Confidence in Valorum's leadership. Tragically, this brave appeal would subsequently lead, much to her surprise, to Senator Palpatine being elected as Chancellor in Valorum's place.

Amidala's magnificent headdress—a striking example of the finery of the Royal House of Naboo—matched her bold words. Gold beads and suspensa ornaments made from delicate orichalc finework adorn a horned escoffiate headpiece resembling a coif, with finial hairtip ornaments to balance—and thus offset—its considerable weight. The Royal Sovereign of Naboo medal, symbolic of the crown and the responsibility of the throne, is positioned centrally for maximum impact.

The gown is a multilayered affair. A crimson robe trimmed with golden, triple-braided soutache with embossed rosettes along the sleeves is worn over

The sheer weight of the elaborate headdress made it arduous for Amidala to wear during long official meetings.

a red gown with gold beading. For Amidala's address to the Senate, these fine garments were largely concealed beneath a peak-shouldered, red-shot-green cloak. If the headpiece was intended to convey the weight of the world of Naboo, it could be said that the cloak, with its two points rising to meet the ends of the former, symbolized Amidala's idealistic determination to shoulder the burden. The final effect was undeniably powerful.

Amidala's dramatic appearance clearly signaled her commitment to her cause. It would have been difficult for any senator, whatever their views, to dismiss her words purely on the basis of her gender and youth. In this spectacular ensemble, the young queen demonstrated her larger-than-life stature with a theatrical bravado befitting the gravity of the situation.

The Naboo were proud artisans and renowned for their elegant aesthetics, as evidenced by both Amidala's robe (left) and the cloak she wore over it (far left).

18

Meson Taloscope

Location: Naboo
Date: 32 BBY

Scientific advances have led to many achievements, such as the cloning technology that created vast, expendable armies for the emerging Empire. In almost every case, these breakthroughs began with the study of life on the microscopic level.

Meson taloscopes can be used for a number of diagnostic analyses on a submicroscopic structural level, especially for medical and engineering purposes. In the days of the Republic they were often found onboard starcruisers utilized by high-ranking travelers.

When Anakin Skywalker was discovered on the sandy world of Tatooine, the Jedi Qui-Gon Jinn tested his belief in the boy's potential as a future Jedi by examining a sample of Anakin's blood. Hoping to confirm his intuitive feelings by securing irrefutable proof, Jinn conveyed the sample to his apprentice, Obi-Wan Kenobi, for analysis by a meson taloscope aboard Queen Amidala's starship. The results left no room for doubt.

The Force is often described as an energy binding all living things. When examined using a meson taloscope, that mystical power may be evident in the smallest droplet of blood. In Skywalker's blood, midi-chlorians—symbiotic organisms that help determine Force sensitivity—were found. Meson taloscopes were calibrated to read levels of up to 20,000 midi-chlorians, but young Skywalker's count was off the charts. All that the Jedi Qui-Gon could determine that day as he peered through his taloscope was that this nine-year-old boy had the highest-known midi-chlorian count ever recorded, even surpassing that of Master Yoda.

Here is where the science ends and the myth of the Chosen One, born to destroy the Sith and bring balance to the Force, begins.

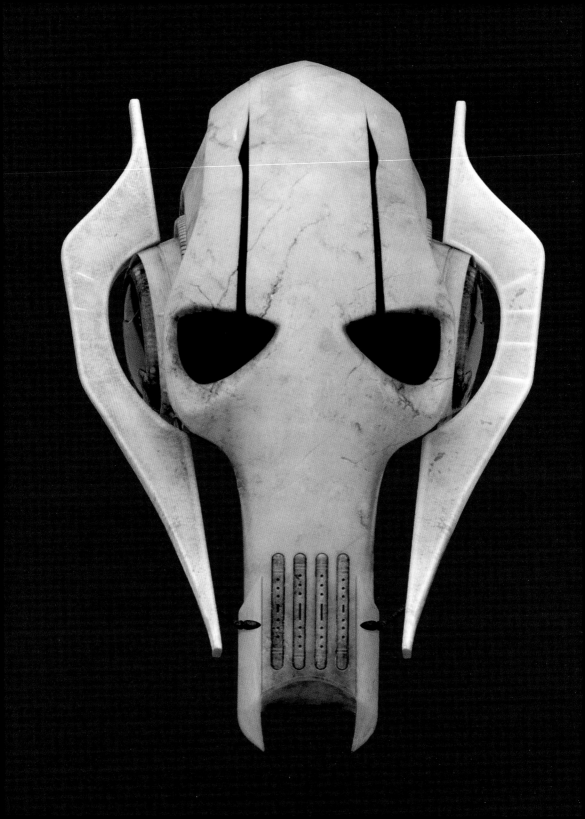

19

The Mask of General Grievous

Location: Vassek
Date: 22 BBY

During the Clone Wars, General Grievous's fortress on Vassek was a veritable shrine to his augmentation as a cybernetic being. A warrior born of the Kaleesh species, by the time he led the Separatist droid army, little remained of his original body. All that his duranium armor contained were his beady eyes, portions of his brain, a pair of damaged lungs, his liver, a few other internal organs, and his cold heart. Ironically, Grievous disdained his purely mechanical militia, perhaps hinting at deeper feelings concerning his own extreme transformation.

It was once thought that Grievous's cybernetic augmentations might have been made against his will. There was speculation that Count Dooku himself, the Sith Lord Darth Tyranus, had orchestrated a shuttle crash that had forced medical droids, under the direction of Darth Sidious, to make the drastic modifications necessary to save the warlord's life.

However, the statues lining the halls of Grievous's fortress tell a different story. In the privacy of his inner sanctum, they appear to trace the history of his transformation, showing the warrior he once was slowly replacing his living flesh with, as he himself termed them, "mechanical improvements." Although Grievous was undoubtedly psychologically conflicted about his final form, there is no evidence that he was a victim of someone else's plot to turn him into a robotic monstrosity.

Regardless of how he came to be, Grievous's cybernetics massively enhanced his abilities, giving him an obvious advantage in battle. His whole body was a weapon, built to deliver precision strikes at a velocity that surpassed his organic muscles. His arms were crafted to resemble the limbs he had been born with, but his hands, instead of possessing four digits, were constructed with six, including two opposable thumbs. Electro-motors activated at a moment's notice could turn his two arms into four thrashing limbs, doubling his strength and effectiveness on the battlefield. Each arm

This statue was located in Grievous's lair on Vassek. It depicts him in his early life: a Kaleesh warrior with a sword in one hand and the severed head of an enemy in the other.

ended in two magnetized talons that enabled him to cling, spiderlike, to the exterior panels of starships or to rapidly scale vertical metal surfaces.

The mask of Grievous paid homage to his earlier life. It mimicked the general shape of his snub nose and the bony protrusions on his chin. It also resembled a Mumuu skull, which Grievous's species once used to wear, smudged with karabba-blood warpaint, when going into battle. Fabricated from durasteel composite duranium, Grievous's armor was not as impenetrable as Mandalorian beskar, yet was far easier to manufacture and to repair.

Grievous's amber eyes peered through his mask, malevolently staring down opponents. Where his teeth should have been, an ultrasonic vocabulator amplified his raspy voice. Owing to his previously impaired lungs, his speech sometimes devolved into coughing fits.

The general fought with a variety of lightsabers despite having no Force-sensitivity or formal Jedi training. The weapons themselves were Grievous's trophies. His impressive, extremely effective fighting style was derived from a combination of training he boasted to have received from Count Dooku and a combat program.

Many Jedi who encountered Grievous on the battlefield were felled by his blade. A notoriously ruthless warrior, he could simultaneously duel with lightsabers and wield a blaster at close range, a deadly double threat for even an experienced, Force-sensitive opponent.

Grievous relished every kill he made, including those of children. In his fortress he kept a collection of the weapons of his victims, along with other souvenirs, such as a macabre case of severed Padawan braids.

During the Clone Wars, damage and defeat forced Grievous to retreat to his home, where his medical droid, EV-A4-D, maintained his implants and armor. With a well-stocked warehouse of new limbs, masks, and other parts, Grievous was able to live for many years, until he was killed by his own blaster on Utapau after a brief altercation with the Jedi Master Obi-Wan Kenobi. It was a fitting, if sad, end for a wretched creature whose obsessive quest for physical prowess and fighting ability rendered him totally unrecognizable to anyone who had ever looked upon his natural face.

20

HB-9 Blaster Rifle

Location: Utapau
Date: 19 BBY

In the three short years that the galaxy was embroiled in the Clone Wars, the Galactic Republic's Jedi generals and their faceless army traversed the stars on countless battlefronts, engaging the Confederacy of Independent Systems from the Core Worlds to the Outer Rim. Those who aligned with either side were equipped with an array of similar weaponry and underwent training to deal with the impending threat.

Some species sought to remain neutral, hoping to rely on their own political ingenuity to stay out of the fight. Yet this position was almost impossible to maintain during the time of the Clone Wars, when many normally peaceful cultures were forced to defend their homeworlds or risk enslavement—or even extinction.

In the waning days of the Clone Wars, the Separatist General Grievous and his forces occupied the planet Utapau, bringing the conflict right to the doors of the indigenous, peace-loving Pau'an race.

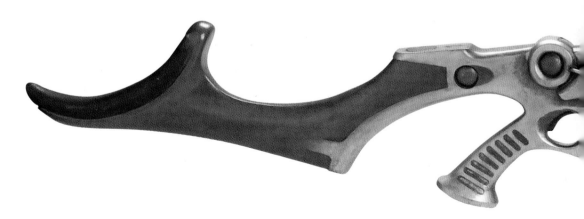

However, the Pau'ans were not completely without their own means of protection. Manufactured by Zenoti Arms, this long rifle is a strikingly artistic piece of machinery. One can easily imagine this ornate blaster prominently displayed on the wall of some high-ranking Pau'an leader's office, a symbolic warning with little likelihood of ever being called into serious aggressive action.

The HB-9 blaster was crafted for long-range combat. A front sight at the end of the barrel helped the user target threats from afar. The hand-turned recharge valve suggests the weapon was made in small batches. Its primitive igniter housing and the archaic priming mechanism behind the trigger housing implies that the rifle was intended more for show than for serious combat. Its elegant stock and shoulder brace, intricate metalwork, and the ring of small jewels embedded along the barrel confirm the impression that this blaster, at least, was used for ceremonial purposes.

The Pau'ans generally believed that a show of authority backed up by impressive-looking HB-9s would prevent a fight from breaking out and keep the peace. This praiseworthy approach was almost always effective among their own kind. Unfortunately, it was of little use when the well-equipped and highly motivated armies of the Separatists, and later of the Galactic Empire, chose to occupy their planet.

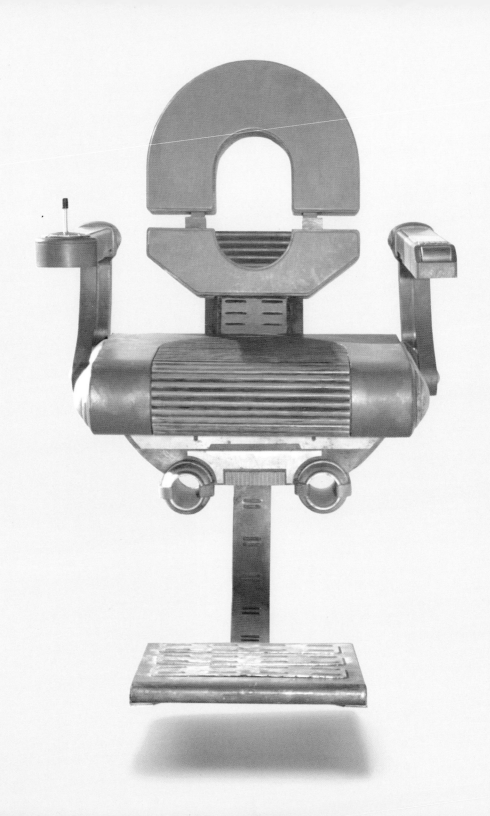

21
Cliegg Lars' Hoverchair

Location: Tatooine
Date: 22 BBY

Toward the end of his life, Cliegg Lars kept watch over his family's land from this hoverchair while mourning the loss of his wife, Shmi Skywalker.

For decades on the arid planet of Tatooine, a few determined and resourceful settlers had eked out an existence near the village of Anchorhead, an oasis amid the the Jundland Wastes and the Dune Sea. Cliegg Lars lived for many years as a moisture farmer there. Utilizing dozens of vaporators to harvest water from the planet's atmosphere, Lars toiled on the same homestead his family had occupied for generations. After losing his first wife and raising their son, Owen, Lars fell in love with Shmi Skywalker, a slave he met on a trip to Mos Espa. Lars purchased Shmi from her Toydarian junk-dealer master, Watto, but the farmer clearly had no intention of keeping her enslaved. Shmi was immediately set free and in time became Lars' second wife. They spent a few happy years together before Shmi went missing one morning while gathering mushrooms from the vaporators.

Lars immediately mounted a rescue attempt to save his beloved, forming a posse of some 30 rugged individuals prepared to take on the Tusken tribe believed to have kidnapped her. But only four survived a counter-raid, and Cliegg himself was badly wounded, his right leg hacked off at the knee. To make matters worse, the Tusken Raiders had spirited Shmi away to their desert encampment and Lars never saw her again.

Rather than incur the expense of a cybernetic prosthesis, Lars took to using a hoverchair. He found it a practical, if not particularly comfortable, substitute for his missing limb. The metal seat could not be adjusted. The only semblance of luxury the chair offered was a footrest for his other leg.

Confined to his hoverchair, Lars spent his last days floating among the sand dunes on his farm. His love for Shmi Skywalker never died.

22

Anakin Skywalker's Cybernetic Arm

Location: Coruscant
Date: 22 BBY

Cybernetic enhancements and droid components are so commonplace that at first glance there would appear to be nothing special about this artificial limb. Its five spindly metal digits are capped with electrostatic fingertips that simulate the feeling of human touch. Exposed wiring, like nerve endings, can be found threaded throughout. Without armored shielding or, at minimum, a glove, this could easily be snagged, severed, or tangled.

The mechno-limb belonged to the Jedi Knight Anakin Skywalker, after his right arm was lopped off in a duel with Count Dooku during the Battle of Geonosis. Given Anakin's talent for mechanical engineering, which gave rise to the protocol droid C-3PO, it is possible that he fashioned it from parts and pieces himself. More likely, the prosthesis was speedily created for him by the physicians of the Grand Army of the Republic. As such, it would have been one of the first of many they constructed to make wounded Jedi fit for the frontlines of war. Over time, the hand was upgraded with a firmer framework and more responsive cybernetic technology.

This particular cybernetic limb undoubtedly had murky origins. It also has greater significance. Anakin was lauded as one of the strongest of all the Jedi, brave in battle, and strongly protective of friends and family. As he was gradually seduced to the dark side, he became the Sith Lord Darth Vader, a cybernetic beast more machine than man. This mechno-arm thus serves as a portent of Anakin Skywalker's grim future.

When the limb was fitted to his still-raw flesh, no one could have guessed that this heroic young man would become a monster. It was assumed that his mechno-arm would allow Anakin to carry on his life more or less normally. For Anakin, unfortunately, his cybernetic prosthesis proved to be just the first of many artificial augmentations that would eventually render him utterly unrecognizable to those he loved.

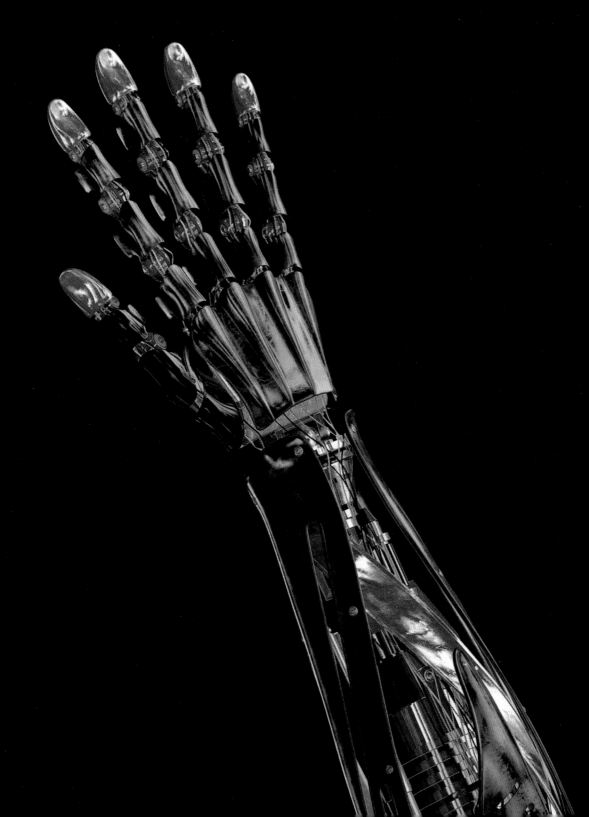

23

Jedi Robes

Location: Coruscant
Date: 19 BBY

There is a revealing subtext in the chosen attire of the Jedi Order. Up until their final days, the Jedi traversed the galaxy in long robes, layered tunics, and tabards, with little personal affectation or adornment. Strikingly similar, the robes of the Jedi were a visible reminder of their ascetic beliefs and their peacekeeping vocation.

In the days of the High Republic, the Jedi maintained pristine white ceremonial robes for formal functions, and more rugged attire for exploring unknown regions of the galaxy and identifying new outposts in need of their protection. Although skilled in combat, the Jedi never aspired to become great warriors. Protectors and peacekeepers, scholars and sages, their role was clear in the monkish silhouette of their clothing.

This set of robes belonged to the Jedi Master Mace Windu, a champion of the Jedi ideals who served as a senior member of the Jedi High Council in the waning days of the Republic. His robes reflect the typical style of dress for those Jedi practitioners who adopted the ancient traditions that had directed their kind for centuries.

Windu was renowned as a legendary duelist, and a decisive and perceptive guiding force among the decision-makers of the day. He heroically fought to protect the Order from interference, indoctrination, and corruption at the hands of the Galactic Senate. Windu was among the first to record concerns about a ripple in the Force that suggested troubling times ahead and a looming darkness. One of the most outspoken critics of Anakin Skywalker's acceptance as a Jedi Padawan, he firmly believed in the Jedi Order's age limits, which required younglings to begin training before they formed attachments that would be difficult to sever in the quest for balanced service to the Force. Windu was a stern teacher who did not suffer fools or students who sought to bend the rules for personal gain.

Even as the Clone Wars swept across the galaxy, Windu strived to protect the Jedi precepts, ultimately failing to maintain the core values of peacekeeping in a climate where he and his brethren were made to serve the Republic as generals and warmongers. Killed in battle with Darth Sidious

just before the execution of Order 66, his robes are a somber reminder of the decades of decisive guidance and strict stewardship Windu provided before he was overpowered by the shadow of the Sith.

At first sight, a lineup of Jedi appeared to be made up of almost identical individuals, their faces concealed in shadow by oversized hoods. In rare cases of combat and conflict, the Jedi's voluminous cloaks provided little in the way of protection, but could make it difficult for an attacker to target their most vulnerable areas.

A few Jedi did buck tradition by dressing in a more distinctive way, but in general their robes were practical, functional, plain, and studiedly undemonstrative, as befitted their vocation. The Jedi devoted their lives to the light side of the Force, rejecting worldly desires of wealth, power, or fame, as well as shunning family and romantic attachments. A Jedi's outer robe also concealed any distinctive features that might define them as being a specific species or gender.

Beneath a heavy outer robe, Jedi clothing was made from humble materials—easily sourced fibers that were functional for travel, if slightly itchy to wear. A tan tunic, tabard, matching pants, and a utilitarian belt created a uniform of sorts.

While royal houses frequently announced themselves with elaborate symbols woven throughout their garments and other clear signs of wealth, such as jewelry, the robes of the Order were significantly lacking in obvious adornments. Yet this lack of decoration certainly did not equate to a dearth of meaning. Their vestments' austere simplicity, with little color, shape, or definition—their deliberate lack of obvious design—was a clear and calculated statement in itself. Their robes set them apart from others, and proclaimed the Order's unworldliness.

For the majority, Jedi robes were a symbol of their sacred vows, and, in their sheer weight, a reminder of their

Anakin's attire was the typically functional clothing of a Jedi Padawan, belying his restless spirit.

responsibilities. From a young age, Padawan learners adopted this simple wardrobe as a symbolic manifestation of their oath to avoid attachments; embrace an existence of spiritual curiosity; and proclaim their intense, unwavering commitment to serving the Force.

However, a particularly distinctive set of robes belonged to the Jedi Knight Barriss Offee, who once served as Padawan to Luminara Unduli. As both women were Mirialan, their robes reflected their culture. Sumptuous fabrics from their home planet showcased their facial tattoos while still conforming with the overall image of the Jedi Order.

Offee's attire's dark color palette is striking and significant given her own sad history as a defector from the Jedi Order during the waning days of the Clone Wars. Disillusioned by what Offee saw as the Jedi Order's fall from grace, in 19 BBY she helped to orchestrate a brutal act of terrorism in her own home. She planted a bomb in the Jedi Temple and framed the Padawan Ahsoka Tano.

Although Offee was ultimately arrested and convicted of the crime by a military tribunal, Tano abandoned the Jedi soon after, disheartened by their poor handling of the incident. At her trial, Offee remained steadfast in her belief that the Jedi and the Republic had both lost their way. Her outspoken pronouncements proved prescient given the final act of Palpatine's master plan, which resulted in the near extinction of the Jedi and the collapse of the Republic.

The robes of the Jedi reminded both those in their presence and the Force-wielders themselves that they lived apart from conventional society. Those deemed most successful among their ranks embodied the lessons of the life-giving energy of the Force and walked the path it alone prescribed.

In honor of her Mirialan heritage, the Jedi Knight Barriss Offee wore a black underdress and a navy-blue cowl, similar in silhouette to other Jedi robes yet unique to her culture.

Imperial Era

The Empire is in the ascendant. Self-appointed Emperor Sheev Palpatine, once the Supreme Chancellor of the Galactic Republic, remakes the galaxy in his own image. Physically scarred and emotionally corrupt, his promises of order are a welcome reprieve for citizens who have survived the turmoil of the Clone Wars.

The people do not resist him when he issues chain codes. They do not defy him when he deploys a new kind of soldier, the stormtrooper, to enforce his rule. Most still do not disobey him when he dissolves the Galactic Senate and takes unlimited power for himself with the unveiling of his Death Star.

Over time, growing unrest gives rise to the Alliance to Restore the Republic, also known as the Rebel Alliance. This development ignites the Galactic Civil War. The few Jedi that remain raise their heads, eyes trained on a new hope for the future.

24

The Skywalker Lightsaber

Location: Coruscant
Date: 22 BBY

Few items are as historically significant as the Skywalker lightsaber. Members of the dynastic family behind the blade can be found intertwined with moments that shaped the galaxy over a 50-year span, from the Clone Wars to the fall of the First Order regime. Three among them carried this particular lightsaber. It was an heirloom passed down through the years as each new generation tried to correct the mistakes of its predecessors.

The 28-centimeter (11-inch) carbon-and-alloy hilt was fabricated by the young Jedi Anakin Skywalker following the loss of his right arm in battle with former Jedi Master Count Dooku, the figurehead of the Separatist movement. While other lightsabers were created to keep the peace, this particular weapon was made with a very different purpose in mind. It was forged in the aftermath of the Battle of Geonosis, which heralded the start of the Clone Wars. As the product of a galaxy on the verge of war, its legacy was sure to sharply diverge from those of previous lightsabers.

Skywalker wielded the weapon in countless battles, deflecting blaster fire and cutting down enemies with irresistible, Force-driven skill. It was the saber of a true hero. The kyber crystal within the hilt yielded a stunning blade of blue, a shaft of light clearly identified in battle as belonging to a Jedi Knight.

However, in the hands of Anakin's dark side alter ego Darth Vader the saber took on a very different aspect. It became the blade that executed dozens of Jedi—Masters, Padawans, and younglings alike—at the Temple on Coruscant as Order 66 ushered in the Empire. If this object could speak through the Force, would it choose to focus on its triumphs or remember its dark deeds?

For nearly two decades, the lightsaber was kept safe by Anakin's Jedi Master, Obi-Wan Kenobi, while he lived a hermit's existence on the sands of Tatooine. The hilt was rightfully Kenobi's after he won a near-fatal duel

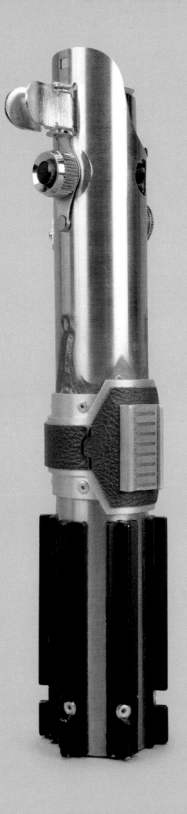

between himself and Anakin on the fiery shores of Mustafar. Buried in the sands of Tatooine alongside Kenobi's own weapon, the two sabers were a sad reminder that the bond of their brotherhood was now irretrievably broken.

The blade was bequeathed to Anakin's son, Luke, by Obi-Wan Kenobi soon after the Rebel Alliance surfaced as a threat to the Empire, following the unveiling of the Death Star and the theft of the battle station's blueprints. With little formal training, Luke Skywalker rapidly became a hero like his father, harnessing the family's blood-born strength in the Force to beat back the darkness the Empire had thrust upon the galaxy. But just as Anakin lost the weapon to Kenobi in their duel on Mustafar, Luke was separated from his inheritance—and his right hand—in a duel with Anakin's alter ego, Vader, on Cloud City.

Luke returned to Cloud City to seek the lost lightsaber, but his search was in vain. Fortunately, it was saved from destruction with the city's garbage,

The ancient pirate Maz Kanata held some of her most prized treasures in this chest, including the legendary Skywalker saber.

but for nearly three decades, the lightsaber's whereabouts was unknown. When it eventually resurfaced, it was being kept by the pirate queen Maz Kanata in an old wooden chest in the depths of her castle on the remote planet of Takodana. How she came by it is a mystery. The Force-sensitive Maz gifted the lightsaber to a scavenger called Rey, recognizing that she was worthy to wield it.

The legacy of this lightsaber's dark past was a topic of much consternation among the surviving Skywalker family members. After tracking down Luke on the remote planet of Ahch-To, Rey tried to return the weapon to Luke, who claimed to have absolutely no interest in revisiting his past or wielding a lightsaber so burdened with blood. At the same time, Ben Solo, having adopted the persona of Kylo Ren, coveted the lightsaber as a link to his idol, Darth Vader.

But some treasures are fated to be preserved. Born to the Palpatine bloodline, Rey used her technical prowess and wisdom gleaned from ancient Jedi texts to repair the lightsaber. She healed the crystal and restored the handle, adding her own personal touch that can be seen joining the carbon hilt once more. She also took on the name Skywalker, in honor of the legacy, and thus prevented the line from dying out with the death of Ben Solo.

The Skywalker lightsaber stands as a reminder that hope can be restored. If the saber could tell its own story, perhaps it would say something like this: Even the most broken among us have a chance to be whole again with the right compassion and care.

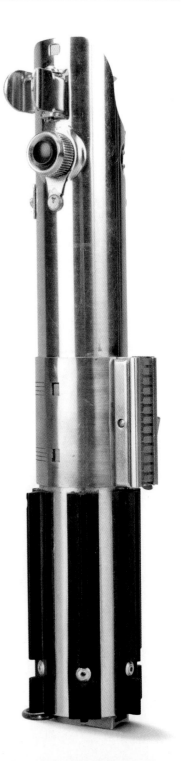

The original Skywalker lightsaber before it was damaged during Luke's Cloud City duel with Darth Vader.

25

Palpatine's Robes

Location: Coruscant
Data: 19 BBY

Empire Day. For devotees of the Imperial regime, a cause for celebration. For those who mourned the loss of the Republic's democratic ways, it was a day that would live in infamy.

Sheev Palpatine has gone by many names and titles through the ages. He could appear benign and unassuming while manipulating those around him to achieve his towering ambitions. In the political arena, Palpatine rapidly rose from being the senator representing Naboo to the Supreme Chancellor of the Galactic Republic. Acting under the guise of his Sith Lord persona, Darth Sidious, he orchestrated the outbreak of the Clone Wars, pushing the galaxy to the breaking point. He deliberately fostered conflict and turmoil to achieve his master plan. For it was only by creating chaos that Palpatine could emerge as the savior of the galaxy, a ruler answering to no one.

Pitting the Republic against the Separatists, Sidious secretly controlled Count Dooku and the sprawling droid army. Meanwhile, in public, Palpatine organized the Republic's clone army, designating the Jedi as the generals who would lead individual legions on the frontlines. Then, after three long years of conflict, Palpatine used the growing wave of public distrust in the sect —once respected as galactic peacekeepers—to paint them as warmongers, hungry for power.

On the first-ever Empire Day, Palpatine delivered an impassioned decree that would mark the last gasp of the Republic. His speech rang out from the chambers of the Galactic Senate across the galaxy via holonet. Palpatine's appearance was as startling as his words. Exhibiting a flair for the dramatic, Palpatine had replaced his usual ceremonial garb for a relatively simple blood-red robe with a velvet cowl. Beneath the hood, onlookers stared spellbound at their leader's distorted face, warped almost beyond recognition after a near-fatal battle with the Jedi. Healthy human flesh had been replaced by a web of ghostly white scar tissue. His eyes were now sunken into the creased flesh. Rimmed in red, their formerly blue irises had turned a blazing, sickly yellow.

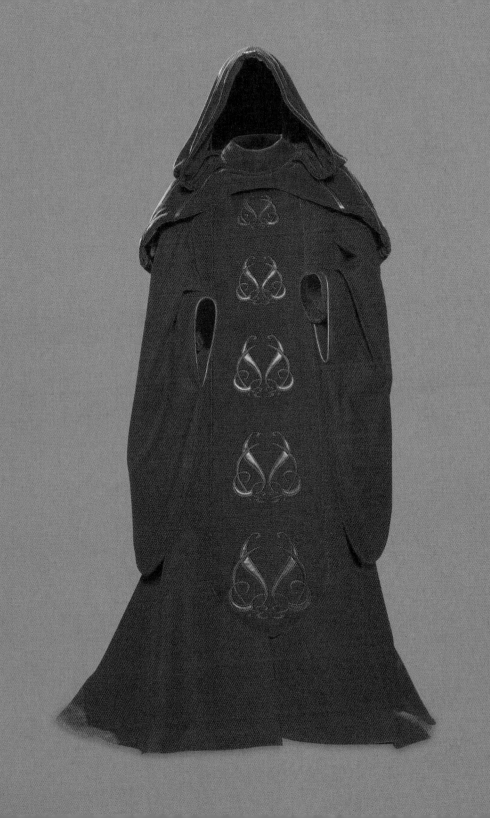

Always one to find an advantageous outcome in almost any situation, Palpatine used his pitiful-looking injuries as evidence of his own narrative that the Jedi Order had rebelled against the Republic they had once sworn to protect. The only possible punishment to fit this appalling act of treason was death. However, Palpatine's speech that day was not a plea for help or sympathy from the populace. It was a victorious rallying cry. "The Jedi rebellion has been foiled," he declared. "In order to ensure security and continuing stability, the Republic will be reorganized into the first Galactic Empire, for a safe and secure society."

With this simple pronouncement—and the secret execution of Order 66 that saw the clone troopers turn against their Jedi leaders—the Clone Wars came to an end. The Republic was dissolved, and in its place Palpatine took his seat as the Emperor of a new age. With the Jedi all but exterminated, Palpatine continued to hide his Sith affiliation, emerging as the figurehead of what many hoped would be a peaceful new era of prosperity. Palpatine fed the public's hunger for protection, employing what remained of his enigmatic smile as he selflessly vowed to lead the Empire and its people. "The attempt on my life has left me scarred and deformed," he admitted, "but I assure you, my resolve has never been stronger."

However, before long, Palpatine's true character emerged as his intentions became inceasingly apparent. Seated on the throne of the Empire, he adopted the black robes of the Sith. He also chose to base himself in the Jedi Temple on Coruscant.

Looking back, as historians trace the events that led to Empire Day, Palpatine's attire seems to suggest a descent into, if not madness, an oblique way of thinking. The people of Naboo are known for

As his secret Sith persona Darth Sidious, Palpatine wore these black robes to conceal his identity. After the fall of the Jedi Order, Palpatine no longer hid in the shadows, donning the cloak in public without fully announcing his position as a Sith Master.

their fashion sense, and his status as a politician on Coruscant dictated that he follow certain decorum and formal dress while representing his homeworld. However, after being named Supreme Chancellor and being granted emergency powers at a crucial moment of crisis—the outbreak of the Clone Wars—Palpatine's wardrobe became more eccentric. By the last phase of the galactic conflict, he had adopted darker and more somber vestments.

On the holonet, some saw Palpatine's garments as a symbol of his empathy. They assumed that his choice of crimson and burgundy fabrics was a deliberate reminder to the public that he carried the weight of the war's bloodshed on his conscience and mourned those lost in combat. It is likely that Palpatine's choice of attire was more accurately a reflection of his bleak outlook. It was the clothing of a dictator figuratively bathing in the blood of those killed in turmoil he had created himself. He was effectively reveling in the atrocities committed in the name of the Republic and keenly aware that, regardless of the outcome of the war, he alone would emerge victorious.

As the years passed, even those once eager to buy into his grandiose promises began to see the fissures forming in the bedrock of his government. It became clear to all but his most fervent followers that his Imperial regime was a system created and controlled by Palpatine himself in order to facilitate his own quest for ultimate power.

While serving as Supreme Chancellor, Palpatine's unfettered power during the Clone Wars all but made the Galactic Senate obsolete. An homage to his homeworld of Naboo, he wore this burgundy ensemble at the end of the conflict.

26

Lando Calrissian's Sabacc Deck

Location: Numidian Prime
Date: 14 BBY

The popularity of sabacc dates back generations and it is one of the most common games played in homes from the Core Worlds to the Outer Rim. The conveniently portable, 62-card deck offers countless variations as a player's skills increase. There are numerous versions of sabacc, from Corellian Spike to Coruscant Shift. Each one has its own special rules.

Most sabacc players learn the basic rules playing with family or friends, where simple bragging rights are all that is at stake. However, the game has also given rise to a veritable empire of professional gamblers—high-rollers playing for big money.

This game is a perfect balance of skill and chance. Each player around the table tries to get to the end of three rounds of gameplay with a hand that equals zero. In addition, every variation of sabacc inherently relies on a player's ability to bluff.

Lando Calrissian found his vocation as a young sportsman hoping to gain fame and fortune at the sabacc tables. With a beaming smile that suggested he was always holding a winning hand and a sense of style that let his opponents know that he was a man of wealth and taste, Calrissian's swaggering air of confidence helped him excel.

He acquired a formidable reputation for beating the odds with his winning streaks, due in part to a hidden green sylop tucked up his sleeve. However his luck ran out on Numidian Prime when he famously wagered his ship, the *Millennium Falcon*, in a hand of sabacc against Han Solo. The young smuggler was aware of Calrissian's trickery and outfoxed him by appropriating his secret card before the game.

27

Main Sensor Rectenna

Location: Endor System
Date: 4 ABY

The *Millennium Falcon* is an object of legend. At various times, the YT-1300 freighter was in service as a tug, a smuggling vessel, and a standout in the Rebel Alliance fleet. In operation for more than 90 years, the *Falcon* was modified countless times to fit the requirements of a rogues' gallery of owners. Records linked to the vessel's serial number, YT 492727ZED, indicate that the freighter was built in the shipyards of Corellia around 60 BBY. Once registered under the name *Stellar Envoy*, the craft was badly damaged in a collision with a bulk freighter soon after the Empire's reign began. It was reconditioned by a salvager and restored with scrapped parts from a YT-1300p. This was the first of many overhauls that would drastically alter the ship's appearance and capabilities.

Lando Calrissian is credited with dubbing the ship the *Millennium Falcon*. The name was retained when Han Solo, and later Chewbacca, took ownership. Merely by focusing on the ship's main rectenna, an essential piece of machinery that controls the vessel's sensor and communications systems, we get an indication of the ship's evolution. While operating as the *Stellar Envoy*, the *Falcon* utilized a military rectenna. A decade later, Calrissian favored a sleek, civilian-model dish, with a more aerodynamic profile. During the age of the Empire, Solo installed a stolen, military-grade rectenna. This round dish was capable of more complex sensor readings and could be linked to a sensor jammer to mask the *Falcon*'s whereabouts—necessary for a smuggler seeking to evade the authorities. It was snapped off during the Battle of Endor and a rectangular CEC rectenna was purchased as a temporary replacement. Given the diminished capabilities of this civilian sensor, it is little wonder that the *Falcon* was stolen from Solo and spent several years changing hands. At this time, the ship was no longer capable of easily detecting potential hijackers, who, aware of the *Falcon*'s exploits, wished to claim the vessel for themselves.

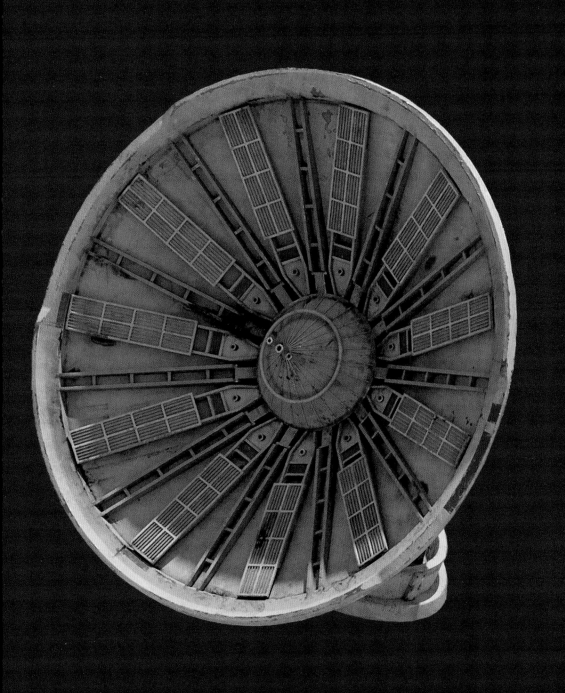

28

Interrogation Droid

Location: Death Star
Date: 0 ABY

Fear kept the Empire in power. Fear of the Empire's wrath, fear of chaos, fear of conflict. Just as the Death Star's arrival signaled a planetary crisis, these spherical droids employed by Imperial interrogators could make even the toughest Rebel tremble in fear.

Developed in one of the Imperial military's top-secret facilities, the interrogator droids employed by the Empire evolved from similar mechanical sentries that patrolled Separatist prisons during the Clone Wars. With the fall of the Republic, the new Imperial regime brought about order by whatever means it felt were necessary. Like other droids who served the Empire, interrogators were utilized to make officers more effective in their duty by snuffing out whatever spark of rebellion might be threatening their corrupt notions of government.

For the upper echelons of the Imperial Navy, an interrogator droid was more than capable of handling the messiest part of their work: extracting secrets from suspected spies. Enabling its organic officers to maintain plausible deniability—or simply providing a tool for more pain than they could or were willing to inflict—an interrogator droid would float ominously into a prisoner's cell bearing a syringe filled with an array of useful medications. From drugs to inhibit pain tolerance, making even slight discomfort utterly unbearable, to truth serums and hallucinogens, the dull hum of an interrogator droid promised one thing: the end of a captive's ability to resist.

29

The Path Safehouse Remnant

Location: Mapuzo
Date: 9 BBY

They called it the Hidden Path. After the enforcement of Order 66, Jedi sympathizers and the scattered survivors of the Order built a secret network to evade capture by the Inquisitorius. Force-sensitive beings hid in safehouses, tunnels, and secret rooms. On the walls of a safehouse on Mapuzo, those who had come before left graffiti. Rough-hewn wood became message boards inscribed with codes and inspiration. In the shadows, hope persisted in the form of scrawled symbols and communiqués.

The Jedi Obi-Wan Kenobi and Leia Organa were among the Force-sensitive refugees to pass through that sanctuary on Mapuzo, destined for Jabiim. The maverick Jedi Quinlan Vos, who helped smuggle younglings to freedom, also used this network. He had boldly left his name so that others in a similar situation might recognize it and be comforted. Vos's act of defiance was a morale-boosting signal to remain hopeful, despite the dangerous times ahead. It was also a defiant recognition that he—like many of those following after—would soon be shedding his old identity and going into hiding.

Other travelers along the Path left enigmatic phrases. "Only when the eyes are closed can you truly see," read one. Another echoed the sentiment of the Jedi Order in its prime: "For Light and Life."

This particular shard, ripped from the wall of a safehouse by the Inquisitorius, shows the symbol of the Jedi Order. Behind the starbird is a saber-like shaft of light, a potent symbol of faith and inspiration.

In 9 BBY, the Hidden Path led to the far-flung world of Jabiim, inside an antiquated sanitation depot. This forgotten facility safeguarded all those who traveled there. Thanks to the work of teams of underground operatives, many Force-sensitive beings found safe passage there and were given food, shelter, and new identities. In time the hope was that they could be transferred offworld to somewhere safer. They could then live out their days in peace, provided they did not attract the Empire's attention by tapping into the Force.

30
Magnetomic Gription Boots

Location: Vandor
Date: 10 BBY

During the Empire's reign, elite soldiers known as range troopers—trained to endure harsh conditions—were stationed on far-flung worlds. On the snowy planet of Vandor, a range trooper detail was posted to guard the 20-T Railcrawler conveyex line, which carried coaxium and other valuable cargo to keep the Empire's fleet running. Guarding the high-speed transport required courage and a certain gastrointestinal fortitude. At the first sign of any threat, range troopers had to spring into action, patrolling the exterior of conveyex trains as they hurtled onward at speeds of more than 80 kph (50 mph).

To perform this dangerous task, each trooper was issued with a pair of magnetomic gription boots. The controls were usually tucked into a matching vambrace. Once activated, the boots' mag-seal grip allowed a trooper to plod securely across the roof of a speeding conveyex. Weighing in at 4.5 kg (10 lbs) per boot, it took considerable effort and training to be able to walk—let alone fight—while wearing them.

The rugged, heavy-duty boots have a somewhat droid-like appearance, with an exposed servomotor assembly at the ankle. Twin lights on each shin give clear readings as the mag-seal grip is activated. The boots' oversize, chunky components appear clumsy, but in reality made it easier for troopers to maintain and repair them without assistance from mechanics. At the top of the front shin, a handle enabled soldiers to carry each boot between shifts or during downtime onboard the busy transport system.

The few soldiers who served in this sub-sector of the Imperial military, such as Captain Denwade Banevans and his squad, were known to be exceptional troopers who relished their work. Thanks in part to their gription boots they not only welcomed trouble, they were well prepared for it.

31

Imperial Code Cylinder

Location: Coruscant
Date: 19 BBY–5 ABY

Maintaining security was of the utmost importance to both the Imperial elite and the Rebel Alliance organizers. In the case of the former, access on bases and space stations was restricted to a select few with the appropriate clearances. Security checkpoints were essential to maintaining clandestine operations, where credentials and specific authorization were verified through the use of special code cylinders. From their appearance, these small metal tubes gave nothing away about what hidden doors and which secret meetings their vital coded intel granted access to.

Issued only to the highest-ranking officers, code cylinders were sometimes tipped in a variety of colors that correlated to the red-and-blue badge insignia of the Empire's elite ranking system. Aside from their access and intel functions, code cylinders were used as another means of indicating rank at a glance. Imperial officers often wore them in small pockets on their uniform jacket. Later, their First Order counterparts favored a series of cloth loops on the chests of their uniform jackets, allowing the cylinders to be displayed in the same manner as ammunition on a bandolier.

Code cylinders also allowed the Empire to keep a watchful eye on officer activity. They provided a log of everything from access points cleared to files read and daily movements aboard a vessel or within another military installation. A quick review of code cylinder records by the Imperial Security Bureau could be used to assess an officer's performance as well as discover any suspicious activity. Rebel spies realized that they could even use them to frame individual officers by cleverly swapping in identical code cylinders or stripping an Imperial of their uniform and donning it as a disguise.

Given the sensitivity of the information code cylinders contained, their loss, either by accident or enemy action, was grounds for severe punishment by the Empire. In certain cases, it could even lead to the officer concerned being sentenced to execution for treason.

32

Holochess Table

Location: Corellia
Date: 10 BBY

When Lando Calrissian owned the *Millennium Falcon,* he took care to make the freighter feel more like a luxury cruiser. His primary objective was gambling his way to a fortune, so the tools of his trade were accoutrements other owners might have thought were taking up precious cargo space, like a holochess table. For Lando, holochess was a form of mental exercise, allowing him to sharpen his wits. When guests boarded his ship and sat down for a

game, he had the perfect opportunity to study their tells and assess if he should engage them in a friendly or financially beneficial match.

The popular game of holochess can be found in homes and starships across the galaxy. It dates back to well before the Republic civil war and has outlasted the Empire, the First Order, and the Final Order. Holochess is both intellectual and brutish, requiring keen strategy to win, yet relying on the often-violent movements of game pieces resembling real and mythological creatures. Even in a friendly game, the holographic combat can get quite fierce, as the Kintan strider, ghhhk, molator, houjix, k'lor'slug, Mantellian savrip, monnok, bulbous, scrimp and ng'ok face off in simulated battle. This table once displayed 10 characters, but the holo displays for bulbous and scrimp are no longer functional.

Gameplay helped scoundrels and outlaws maintain the intellectual acuity to cope with their dangerous lifestyles. The tiny, monstrous gladiators also provided a safe way to settle disputes without resorting to violence. However, not every species could easily separate the game from real life—which is why it is generally accepted that if playing holochess with a Wookiee, it is always best to let the Wookiee win.

Top to bottom: Kintan strider, Mantellian savrip, and molator holochess pieces.

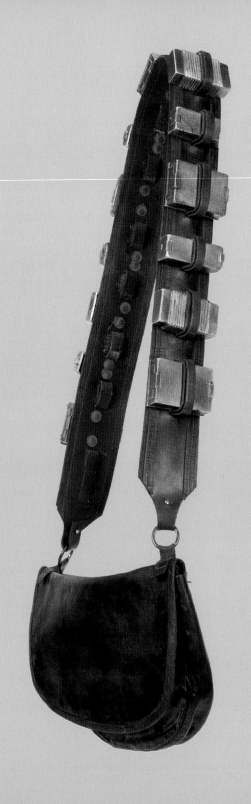

33

Chewbacca's Bandolier

Location: Kashyyyk
Data: 19 BBY

The Wookiee Chewbacca was born in the city of Rwookrrorro, near the tree-city of Kachirho where the noble beings defended their homes during the last months of the Clone Wars. Although Chewbacca, "Chewie" to his friends, was integral in staving off a Separatist invasion, he could not help his planet avoid Imperial occupation, which resulted in the devastating enslavement of his species.

In his younger years, Chewie explored the dense forests of his Kashyyyk homeworld, before his restless nature inspired him to voyage to the stars alongside his friend, Han Solo. He was thus at the forefront of some of the most important battles against the Empire.

Whether hunting for game on Kashyyyk or fighting for the Rebel Alliance, Chewie invariably carried a bandolier, leaving his hands free to use weapons. This was modeled after the ammo halter harnesses favored by the Wookiee military, and also resembled some of the Wookiee clans' ceremonial attire. As he crested the 200-year mark, Chewie favored a simple sling style, worn across one shoulder.

Chewie's bandolier—considerably shorter than most, as Chewie was small for a Wookiee even at 2.28 meters (7.5 feet)—typically included a large pouch for essentials, such as his dismantled bowcaster. Crafted from animal hide, the bandolier served a variety of functions. Small metal boxes lined the sash-style strap. These were secured by leather bands that could be adjusted to fit ammunition cells and other items. In times of strife, these boxes contained power packs, blaster gas canisters, and bowcaster quarrels. For lengthy hunts or deployments, they held ammunition, tools, and rations.

The boxes also served to conceal their contents, making it impossible for an enemy to know if his bandolier was stocked with vital ammo or not. Given Chewie's capacity for compassion and sentimentality, it is likely he also carried some personal trinkets. Perhaps one of them might have been a piece of sacred wroshyr wood to remind him of home.

34

Restraining Bolt

Location: Kessel
Date: 11 BBY

Among the galaxy's technologically advanced civilizations, droids were a regular feature of life. They performed a multitude of functions, including agricultural labor, working in the service industry, translating and interpreting foreign languages for dignitaries, and computing calculations to aid starship navigation. Certain factions, including the Empire, used droids for more controversial tasks, like torture and interrogation.

Campaigns to abolish droid servitude were rare; those in favor argued that droids were constructed to serve and nothing more. However, degrees of sentience identifiable within some droids' circuitry presented a counter-argument. In addition, the long-term placement of droids within family units and on military frontlines also led to changes in prevailing attitudes. Some individuals came to regard these mechanized creations as beings with thoughts and feelings. However, a droid that enjoyed a certain degree of freedom and even friendship from its organic masters could easily be compelled to blindly serve another party with a restraining bolt.

At first glance, this small cylindrical device looks like it could be any nondescript droid component, perhaps part of a locomotion-system controller. When installed, it could turn even the most seemingly advanced droid into an automaton. Paired to a small device dubbed a "caller," restraining bolts constrained a droid's functionality to fit a new master's liking. A droid controlled by such a device would have no choice but to cease all other tasks and report immediately to whomever held the controls. Most callers had three basic commands: "Come," "Halt," and "Orders," the last of which compelled the droid to carry out a spoken command. More sophisticated restraining bolts had a wider range of controls.

For droids like C-3PO, who had a deep-seated "sense of self" and were unaccustomed to being regarded as robotic slaves, the effect of a restraining bolt was akin to horror. However, in more responsible hands, a restraining bolt could be utilized to prevent a rogue droid rampage, or a damaging uprising, or to deter a curious astromech—such as R2-D2—from wandering off to pursue its own agenda.

35

Case of Coaxium Vials

Location: Savareen
Date: 10 BBY

In the early days of what would become the Rebel Alliance, a splinter cell of dissidents struggled to find the resources to mount an effective revolt against the menacing Empire. When the uprising was still in its infancy, it was literally fueled by tiny vials of coaxium such as these. They were easily hidden, yet capable of propelling a small fleet of Rebel starships into hyperspace and thus evading the Empire's much more powerful fleet.

Hyperfuel such as coaxium is extremely volatile. Found on the ore-rich mining world of Kessel, this raw hypermatter was a constant danger to those both on the surface and beneath it, if the proper storage protocol was not followed to keep it cool and free from agitation. These coaxium vials are perfectly stable, thanks to the technology on the world of Savareen where, along with countless identical vials, they were produced.

In the underworld markets, the sale of just a few hundred milligrams of coaxium could make the seller a millionaire overnight. Those willing to pay such a fee were often dangerous and powerful criminals. While selling hypermatter could bring an individual immense wealth, entire civilizations might well pay a high price for the transaction.

For the Rebel cause, in the time before the Galactic Civil War fully broke out, coaxium was essential. To quote the Cloud-Rider gang leader and rebel Enfys Nest, the hyperfuel was "the blood that brings life to something new."

Largely thanks to the wiles and courage of Han Solo and Chewbacca, a shipment originally intended for the brutal Crimson Dawn crime syndicate was hijacked and delivered to the fledgling Rebellion. The rest is history.

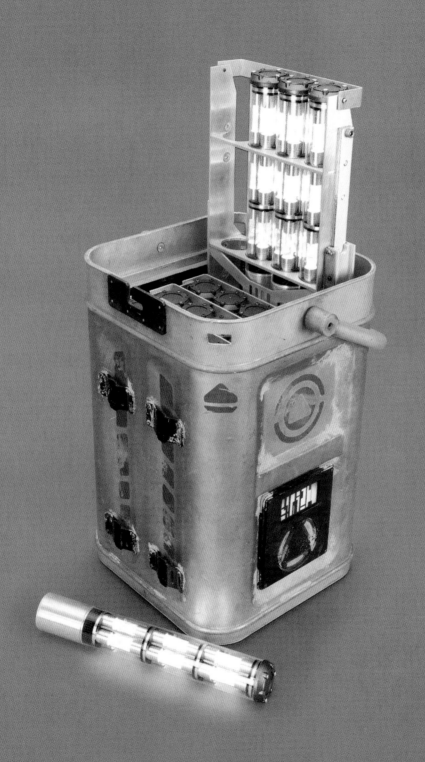

36

Death Star Plans

Location: Scarif
Date: 1 BBY

They called it "Project Stardust." For nearly 20 years, the Empire had steadily expanded its reach, occupying planets, and even creating some semblance of governmental function from the turmoil of the Clone Wars. But in secret, the real work was being conducted in the atmosphere above the planet Geonosis. There, Imperial masterminds were building one of the most staggering superweapons ever conceived—a space station ominously dubbed the Death Star. This sinister plan had been in progress even as the first Clone War battles were breaking out, around 22 BBY.

The size of a small moon, the Death Star contained a superlaser powered by a hypermatter reactor. Upon ignition, the reaction was filtered through eight massive kyber crystals, allowing a focused beam of pure energy to devastate any target. When fully operational, entire planets could be destroyed, species exterminated, and all opposition to the Empire crushed.

The Rebel Alliance looked on helplessly as the the Death Star demonstrated its power by obliterating the holy city of Jedha. It finally appeared to many fighters that the Empire was now all-powerful and could never be defeated. But hope can flicker in the darkest of situations. The Rebel Jyn Erso knew that hidden somewhere within the Death Star's systems lay a flaw, a weakness. This had been implanted by the weapon's chief designer, Galen Erso, Jyn's peace-loving father, a scientific genius whom the Empire had forced to work on the project.

On the tropical world of Scarif, the Empire had erected a vault to protect its greatest military secrets. This installation was heavily fortified. It was protected by elite stormtroopers, and surrounded by deflectors as well as a shield gate high above the planet that barred entry to the surface. Despite these formidable defenses, a Rebel cell led by young Jyn Erso calling itself Rogue One made a successful incursion. While the main party engaged the stormtrooper guards, Jyn and two of the Rebels penetrated the heart of a

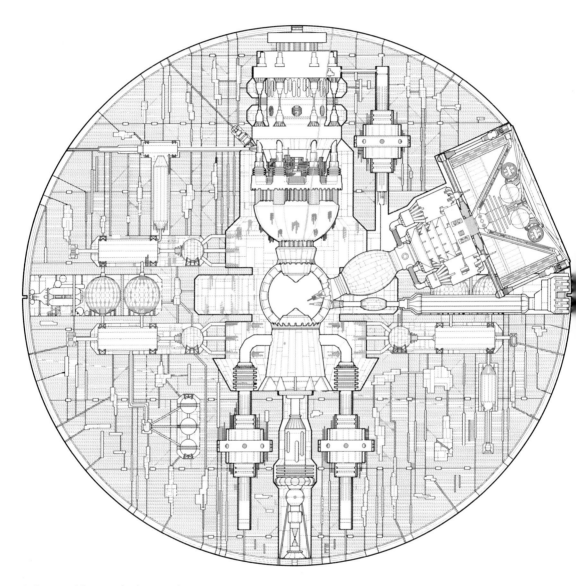

A diagram of the complex inner systems
of the Death Star.

datatree. Among the thousands of identical data cartridges, they found the key to unraveling the Empire's greatest threat.

The datatapes favored by the Empire were large and unwieldy. Their military-grade, shockproof, polyplast casings, and electromagnetic shielding protected everything from databank archives and top-secret files to primary schematics for clandestine projects. In the Structural Engineering node, the entire history of the Death Star's creation was committed to a single cartridge, filling much of its 512-million exanode capacity. Pinpointing the precise location of the flaw, located somewhere within the Death Star's network of heat exchanges and exhaust ports, would require further research by Rebel Alliance scientists.

Before the Rogue One Rebels could escape Scarif with the cartridge, the Imperial facility was destroyed by a single reactor ignition strike—a defensive maneuver carried out by the very weapon the rebels were investigating. By exploiting the Empire's own advanced technology, Jyn Erso and her Rogue One band managed to transmit the plans to the Rebel Alliance just before the base was razed, sacrificing their lives in the process. The most important file—containing Galen Erso's deliberate design flaw—had been copied to a small disc. This was later installed in the memory banks of the war veteran and astromech droid R2-D2.

Not long after the Battle of Scarif, equipped with this intel, the Rebel Alliance launched an attack on the Death Star in the Yavin system. Thanks to the almost unbelievable precision of one X-wing pilot—a young man named Luke Skywalker—the Rebels destroyed the superweapon. None of the Rebels' future victories against the Empire would have been possible without Jyn Erso's Rogue One team's daring operation to snatch that precious datatape cartridge from the Imperial archives.

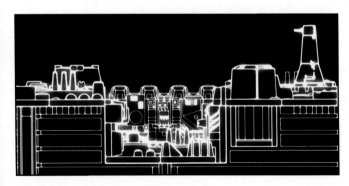

This blueprint shows the meridian trench that the X-Wings flew down. It led to the thermal exhaust port that was their ultimate target.

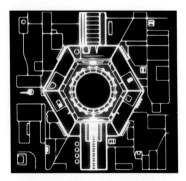

A close-up of the thermal exhaust port that led directly to the Death Star's main reactor.

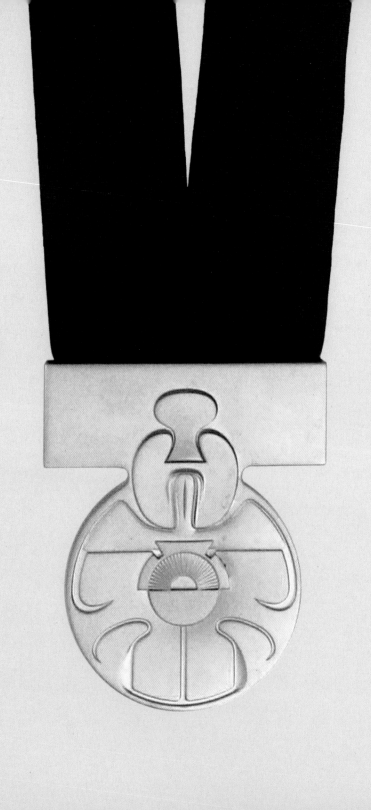

37

Medal of Yavin

Location: Yavin 4
Data: 1 ABY

The Imperial regime temporarily faltered following the destruction of the Death Star during the Battle of Yavin, but high-ranking Rebels knew that this pivotal victory was only the start. In order to win the war and overthrow the Empire, they needed to increase their numbers and influence public opinion against the dictators running the government. To help achieve these aims, the Rebel Alliance needed to create some heroes.

In the brief calm after the clash—which saw many brave Rebel pilots killed in the line of duty—two rogues were awarded medals for their heroics: Luke Skywalker and Han Solo. In a ceremony led by Leia Organa, both new recruits became decorated war heroes. Forged from precious metals, their medals were engraved with a rising sun at the heart of a floral motif. This symbol evoked new beginnings, rebirth, and the resilience to continue the struggle. Hanging from a dark brown ribbon, the award was a throwback to the days of the Republic, when great achievements were formally recognized by the Galactic Senate.

This medal belonged to Han Solo, a reluctant rebel who went on to become a general in the later years of the conflict. The rise of the First Order led to Solo's death at the hands of his son Kylo Ren during the Battle of Starkiller. However, the honor was kept close by Solo's wife, Leia, the woman who had first hung it around his neck, grateful for his willingness to sacrifice himself for the greater good.

Following her passing on Ajan Kloss, the decoration was gifted to Solo's closest friend, Chewbacca the Wookiee. Although Wookiees do not set much store in trophies and trinkets, Han Solo's Yavin medal was a welcome reminder of the special bond the two had shared during their years adventuring around the galaxy.

38

Jyn Erso's Stormie Doll

Location: Lah'mu
Date: 13 BBY

From its inception, the Empire's propaganda machine sought to turn its warmongering agenda into something that appeared more benign. Toy stormtrooper dolls were a subtle, innocuous-seeming way to persuade a new generation of youngsters that the Imperial regime was a freedom-loving force for good.

Recovered from the Erso homestead on Lah'mu, this stormtrooper doll once belonged to Jyn Erso, the daughter of the Imperial scientist Galen Erso and his wife, Lyra. With 13 points of articulation, the toy attempted to present the Imperial military as heroic, even playful. Carved from wood and nicknamed "Stormie" by the young Jyn, the doll was painted to match the white armor of the Empire's infantry, down to the frozen features of its bucketlike helmet.

In the age of the Empire, merchants across the galaxy stocked their shelves with varieties of these figures made from cloth, wood, and other materials. Stormtrooper dolls provided comfort; in effect, they were avatars for children's vivid imaginations.

These playthings also had a more sinister import. They were the first of many increasingly overt messages that sought to drive up enlistment numbers by encouraging children to envision a future for themselves among the Empire's elite troops.

In Jyn's case, the doll's potential propagandist purpose failed utterly. Although the toy was supposed to present the soldiers of the Empire as friendly figures worthy of admiration, Jyn grew up to become an outlaw, fiercely opposed to the Empire's tyranny. She was known by several aliases, before she was killed at the Battle of Scarif, bravely sacrificing her life for the Rebel cause.

39

Probot

Location: Outer Rim
Date: c. 3 ABY

In addition to its mighty force of stormtroopers, the Empire also relied on a small army of probe droids. These probots were prominent among the technological devices dispatched throughout the galaxy to aid the war effort and quash the Empire's enemies. This was particularly true following the Imperial defeat at the Battle of Yavin. Probot strikes nearly resulted in the destruction of the Rebel cause

The rugged design of the Viper probe preferred by the Empire was crafted with deep-space exploration in mind. It included a free-spinning head unit fitted with state-of-the-art sensors that gave the appearance of bulbous eyes; a variety of instrumentation implemented in four or more spindly arms; and recording equipment to relay information back to its operator. The Inquisitorius kept an arsenal of probe droids it could launch from its headquarters on Nur.

The assignments these droids were sent on ranged from reconnaissance and scientific study to military applications and even private investigation. It is easy to imagine a high-ranking Imperial, suspicious of a threat to their person, borrowing a droid for a secret operation.

Programmed to stop at nothing in performance of their missions, probe droids scoured entire planets in search of their targets. Some probot units were fitted with blasters and shielding to prevent them being destroyed or deactivated and reprogrammed by enemies of the Empire.

Despite the droids' effectiveness and their ability to quickly transmit their findings—chirping in omnisignal unicode, a special dialect rattled off over the constant hum of their repulsorlifts—they were considered disposable by the Imperial military.

At one time, 100,000 Vipers were dispatched across the galaxy in the Empire's hunt for Rebel cells. If a probot encountered more powerful opposition, a self-destruct sequence would activate. This was specifically designed to eliminate the threat and also any possibility of salvaging the droid's components for future Rebel use. Given this hardwired destructive feature of the droids' circuitry, it is rare to find an intact, deactivated probe.

40

T-16 Skyhopper Model

Location: Various
Date: 9 BBY

Skyhoppers were a favorite vehicle among young Imperial-era pilots with a zest for speed. These high-performance airspeeders were manufactured in large numbers by the Incom Corporation, part of an array of civilian and military-grade craft that included some of the foremost starfighter models in the galaxy. During the height of the Empire, Incom's models could be found on most habitable planets.

A trio of wings evenly spaced along a triangular hull allowed these small personal speeders to reach impressive speeds. Generations of future fliers credited their first training to the craft. Capable of reaching a planet's troposphere, airspeeders gave young crew members the thrill of exploration without ever really leaving home.

Many youngsters developed a fascination for skyhoppers long before they reached the age of actually being able to fly them. To capitalize on this, toymakers manufactured scale models of the T-16, providing hours of fun for children of all ages. Obi-Wan Kenobi bought one from a Jawa scavenger as a present for Luke Skywalker. It was confiscated by Luke's guardian, Owen Lars, who told Kenobi to stop bringing the boy presents. Lars was well aware that these models captured youngsters' imaginations, encouraging them to dream of one day leaving their homes to take the helm of their very own starship. Mindful of Luke's real father's past as a pilot and Jedi, Lars wanted to keep Luke's feet firmly on the ground.

Some Outer Rim children—including Luke, who nearly killed himself on a reckless burnout run through Tatooine's Beggar's Canyon—learned to pilot these dangerous machines. Whether in the passenger seat, at the controls, or in bed dreaming about a day when they might fly to other worlds, the T-16 skyhopper gave many youngsters the ambition to soar.

41

Chirrut Îmwe's Lightbow

Location: Jedha
Date: 1 BBY

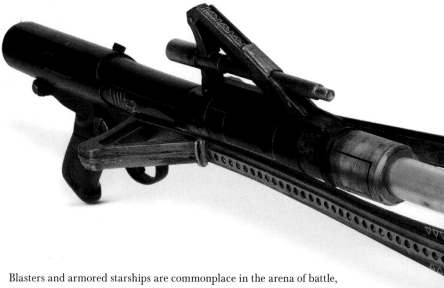

Blasters and armored starships are commonplace in the arena of battle, but some weapons are particularly remarkable for their ingenuity and artisanship. One example is this lightbow, handcrafted by a Guardian of the Whills named Chirrut Îmwe on the Mid Rim moon of Jedha.

Îmwe was a deeply spiritual man and a formidable warrior. He was one of the last surviving protectors of the Temple of the Kyber in the Holy City on Jedha. Whether he came into the world sightless or went blind during his life is unknown.

In combat, Îmwe favored a staff made from the wood of the sacred uneti tree for close-quarters work and, for long-range action, a traditional lightbow.

These handmade weapons were primarily used for defense. They enabled a Guardian of the Whills like Îmwe to preserve the sanctity of their holy land from trespassers, marauders, and thieves. Traditionally, each lightbow signified the attainment of physical perfection on this plane of existence and was created to mark a practitioner's completion of the seventh duan. Comprising parts from an E-11 blaster and folding, artistically etched polarizer limbs, the lightbow was the ultimate symbol of the life of a Guardian of the Whills. Form and functional firepower merged with the beauty of handcrafted artistry. For a Guardian, the very creation of the weapon was a meditative practice on the path to enlightenment.

The Guardians of the Whills were fundamentally peacekeepers inspired by the legendary Jedi Knights of old. Despite having no Force abilities, they were devout believers in the cosmic energy.

Much like the Jedi, the Guardians were aware that the galaxy cannot always be at peace. The lightbow, along with other weapons, helped to reconcile them to this reality, but was intended as a last resort when all other measures had failed. It was far more powerful than a standard heavy rifle. Capable of firing 50 rounds from a standard ammunition power cell, it could bring down a small starfighter. In Chirrut Îmwe's hands, a lightbow could defeat nearly any enemy who refused peaceable requests to back down.

42

Darth Vader's Meditation Chamber

Location: *Executor*
Date: 3 ABY

While bacta tanks remain one of the foremost methods for wound care, this treatment has its limitations for especially debilitating injuries. Where science fails, spiritualism intervenes. Built to provide palliative care and temporary relief rather than lasting healing, this meditation chamber once served as an oasis of calm and command center for the Imperial enforcer Darth Vader.

The specially designed pod was the only place to give Vader relief from the constrictions of his cybernetic armor, and perhaps the only place where he found a modicum of peace. A mechanism in the top section operated pincers that released him from his viselike headgear. They lifted his helmet, then the topmost portion of his mask, and connected its breathing apparatus to a recharging station. The Sith Lord could recline in the pod for as long as he wished, surrounded by a high-pressure gas mixture that safely aired a few precious inches of the web of mutilated flesh that covered his body. This artificial atmosphere, pumped into the chamber through a series of tubes and a carefully calibrated compressor, provided his scarred lungs with a plentiful supply of life-sustaining oxygen. Other transfusions and nutrient supplements could be added as needed.

Although the chamber, as its name suggests, was a place for quiet contemplation, Vader's work as the Emperor's right hand did not cease during his periodic retreats there. Communications consoles and data feeds connected him with his highest-ranking officers at a moment's notice. His helmet could be fitted back into place at the push of a button.

Surrounded by pristine white walls, like a mechanized eggshell protecting a hatchling, Vader could calm his mind and connect with the Force. He could also attempt to reach the last shred of humanity still residing in the black heart of one of the Empire's cruelest servants.

43

Kyber Crystal

Location: Ilum
Date: Unknown

A proverb oft repeated by the Guardians of the Whills, devoted servants of the ancient religious order that once served the Temple of the Kyber on Jedha, used to run thus: "The strongest stars have hearts of kyber."

The rare living crystal is found across the galaxy, from the caves of Ilum to the mines of Utapau. Sacred to the Jedi in particular, who dedicated their lives to using the Force in the defense of peace and justice, these crystals sing in harmony with the energy binding all life.

Kyber crystals had many uses. They powered the lightsabers of the Jedi, focusing the energy of the Force into each blade. Artisans fashioned necklaces from the crystal, believing in its restorative and protective powers. Others created statues from it, sculptures sadly now lost to time. In addition, the Empire's industries strip-mined entire planets and harnessed the kyber deposits they found for machines of war.

Pure kyber is colorless and luminous, resonating with the Force. An intricate latticework shapes each crystal into a unique gem that can never be duplicated in nature or cultured in a lab. Untampered kyber crystals can exhibit something close to consciousness, and one who truly respects the crystal's agency, whatever it may be, may harmoniously work with it, capitalizing on its most useful properties.

Kyber crystals respond to those who claim them. The bond between Jedi Knight and crystal resulted in a specific hue—usually blue—emanating from a Jedi lightsaber's plasma blade.

The kyber crystals used by the Sith and other dark side users made their lightsaber blades glow a sickly red. The Empire also used kyber crystals to power its ultimate superweapon, the Death Star. However, the Empire's corruption does not define the sacred hearts of kyber, and the Death Star was ultimately destroyed by Rebel forces.

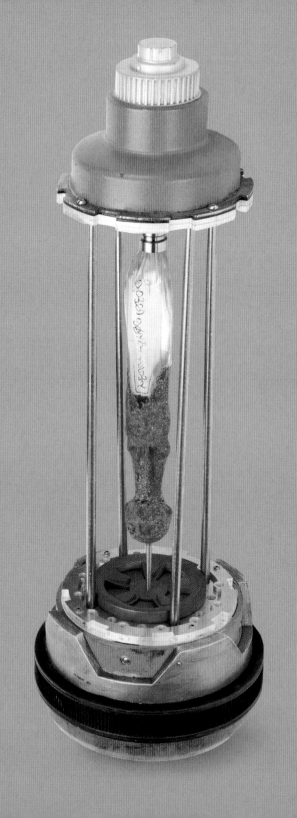

44

Yoda's Blissl

Location: Dagobah
Date: 4 ABY

Devout practitioners of the Force such as Jedi Master Yoda existed in a state of political and personal neutrality in an effort to achieve balance in all things. Although accurate, this depiction fails to take into account the feelings and personalities of individual Jedi students and masters. Some of them formed close bonds, despite avowedly relinquishing attachments and filled their days with more than just studying Jedi teaching, practicing lightsaber forms, and stacking rocks.

The Jedi Master Yoda is one of the most storied of all the Jedi, due in part to his tenure training younglings for approximately 800 years—a staggering term that put him at 900 years old at the time of his death in 4 ABY.

Yoda's final years were spent in exile on the marshy world of Dagobah, where he eked out a humble existence in a hut fashioned from mud bricks and stone built into the base of a gnarltree. In those 20 years of seclusion, he foraged for food, and relied on nature to provide both the rootleaf for his stews and the gimer twigs he used to fashion canes to help him to walk. Dagobah's lush ecosystem, strong in the Force, also provided him with the means to create this blissl.

This tiny pipe instrument from his days of isolation suggests that Yoda instinctively understood the psychological benefits of creating an artifact and experiencing a moment of joy, despite the widespread turmoil afflicting the galaxy. It's intriguing to think of Yoda, always deeply in touch with the Force, alone on Dagobah yet surrounded by a landscape teeming with life, and finding some solace in music. Perhaps, during his final days, Yoda would have essayed a tune on the blissl, adding his own melody to the chorus of the natural world around him.

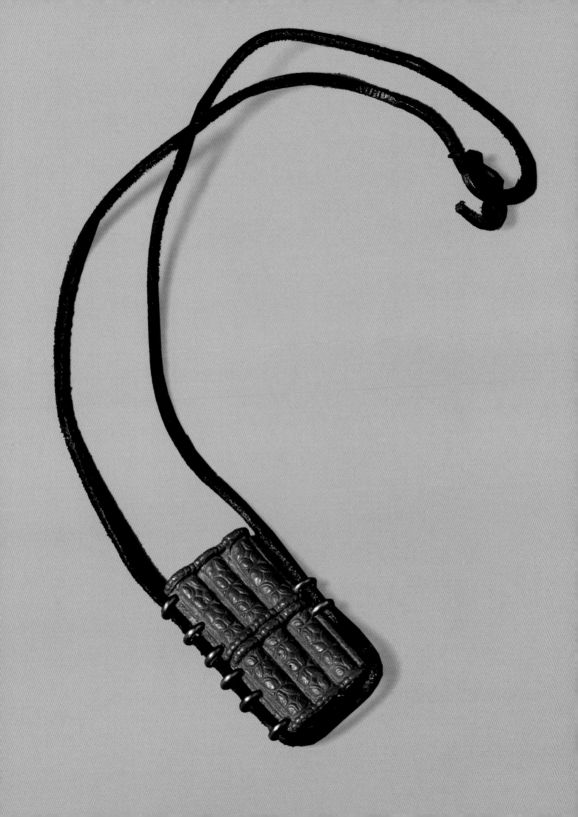

45

Defender Sporting Blaster

Location: Alderaan
Date: 0 BBY

This sleek Defender sporting blaster was created by the Drearian Defense Conglomerate for small-game hunting and self-defense. In the hands of the Rebel Leia Organa, however, the firearm became inextricably linked to the freedom fighters of the Rebellion and the courage and tenacity the last Princess of Alderaan came to represent.

Organa learned how to shoot using a Defender during her teenage years as she rose to prominence and took an interest in galactic politics. By the time she was 19 years old, she was a full-fledged member of the Galactic Senate. Among diplomats and nobility, the Defender was the most commonly used sidearm. This was primarily due to its design. Compact and light, it could be easily dismantled and concealed in pockets or possessions in order to pass undetected through security scans. The blaster was also simple to reassemble, an advantage in the field of espionage and on battlefronts across the many star systems embroiled in the Galactic Civil War.

After Alderaan's annihilation by the Empire's Death Star, Leia often carried some variant of a Defender concealed among her robes. This was perhaps in part because it reminded her of home; the weapon's reliability, slim silhouette, and other user-friendly features were also factors.

With a power cell allowing 100 shots per charge, the blaster was a practical sidearm during a firefight, especially for a skilled shooter. A stun feature could disable an enemy for interrogation, instead of seriously wounding or killing them.

Leia's blaster was both a tool of rebellion and a symbol of hope. It was a crucial part of her unwavering commitment to the cause of democracy, which Leia would one day be integral in reinstating throughout the galaxy.

46

Protocol Droid Head

Location: Tatooine
Date: 5 ABY

The head of a protocol droid served up on a platter was the gruesome sight that greeted visitors to crime lord Bib Fortuna's palace during his brief reign. It was a stark warning to those bringing Fortuna bad news. His predecessor, Jabba the Hutt, was likewise renowned for taking his anger out on his servants. In at least one case, he disintegrated a protocol droid when displeased with the interpreter's message.

Primarily manufactured by Cybot Galactica on the world of Affa, the 3PO series model was popular for several decades. The standard humanoid body could be fitted with various heads to suit a particular culture. The basic model was equipped with more than six million forms of communication, with an upgradable databank and memory modules.

Due to the prevalence of the 3PO series model, junkyards and market stalls often featured spare parts. Hobbyists could also purchase kits to build their own from scratch. The core personality chip was implanted in the head, along with other sensitive data that helped to give each unit a unique personality. The 3PO series was available in a variety of finishes, from bronzium gold to a metallic-flecked crimson.

On Core Worlds like Coruscant, protocol droids performed the essential functions of translation and diplomacy during political debates and business negotiations. When survival took precedence over etiquette, 3PO droids assisted in the management of workhorse droids and even provided some semblance of companionship. On Tatooine, they served in both roles. Young Anakin Skywalker built his mother a protocol droid from parts found in their home city of Mos Espa. Anakin's droid, C-3PO, would become a hero of the Rebellion, but others—like the interpreter serving the irascible Bib Fortuna—were not so fortunate in their affiliations.

47

Astromech Tools

Location: Naboo
Date: 40 BBY

Astromech droids are found throughout the galaxy. Hardwired to serve primarily as pilots, navigators, and mechanics, each one is a unique representation of the engineer who built it and a reflection of its master's needs. What distinguishes these droids from their counterparts functioning in the realm of protocol and other specialties is the array of tools contained inside their compact bodies.

Beneath an astromech's dome, a holographic projector provides a standard means of communication, alongside an onboard logic function display and a telescoping scanner like the one illustrated. This hardware is connected to an internal interface that potentially gives a droid the ability to scan great distances and act as a portal to relay messages.

A pair of arms and a telescopic leg protruding from beneath its cylindrical bodies keep an astromech upright. These features are common to the older C-series models still found operating in far-flung corners of the galaxy as well as the more predominant R series.

Inside an astromech, hidden behind the many panels found around its durasteel carapace, are the right tools for almost any task. Some situations required a droid to employ more than one tool and also to problem-solve at speed. An astromech's remarkable ability to select just the right tool at the right time allowed it to work efficiently without detailed instructions from a sentient master.

The heroic war hero R2-D2, who stands out among the most revered astromech droids of his class, had no fewer than 20 tool arms for probing, cutting, and grasping. At a moment's notice the droid's numerous sensors and scanners would assess damage to a ship or another droid and choose the appropriate tool to fix the problem. However, given the unpredictable nature of combat situations, there were some cases that called for Artoo to make extremely quick calculations and use considerable ingenuity. This often involved using his gadgetry in ways not necessarily intended by the manufacturer. For example, the primary purpose of Artoo's shock prod was to solder together metal parts when making repairs. However, after Leia

Organa slayed Jabba the Hutt with the chains he had used to hold her prisoner, the trusty droid employed that same arm twice to help himself and his friends escape. The gadget's powerful electric current swiftly severed Organa's shackles and freed her from captivity. The same tool was then powered down and used to jolt a Kowakian monkey-lizard that was pestering the droid C-3PO. A single zap sent the creature scurrying and prevented Artoo's close friend from losing essential parts.

Some droids employed short-range rocket thrusters to traverse rough and rocky terrain, or to provide a boost to lock into the droid socket on a small starfighter. On at least one occasion, Artoo evaded capture by emptying his oil reserves and igniting the lubricant with the exhaust from his thrusters to create a sudden blaze. Like his other tools, his thrusters were safely ensconced in hydraulic arms to prevent them from being damaged or even knocked off.

In the final days of the Clone Wars, when Obi-Wan Kenobi and Anakin Skywalker had been arrested by the Separatist General Grievous aboard his flagship the *Invisible Hand,* Artoo famously decided to deploy all of his numerous gadgets at once in order to fake a total system malfunction. Waving his arms and emitting a high-pitched squeal, his antics distracted Grievous's guards and allowed Kenobi to free himself from his restraints. Artoo's quick thinking makes a sound argument as to why one should never underestimate an astromech droid.

A single bulb powers this standard holoprojector, used to display three-dimensional images and schematics as well as prerecorded messages.

Among the array of armlike tools kept in an astromech's panels are (top to bottom): a shock prod; a basic repair arm for interfacing with starship tech; a gas torch; a standard two-pronged grasper; a terminal interface probe; and a polydigital grasper for more detailed work.

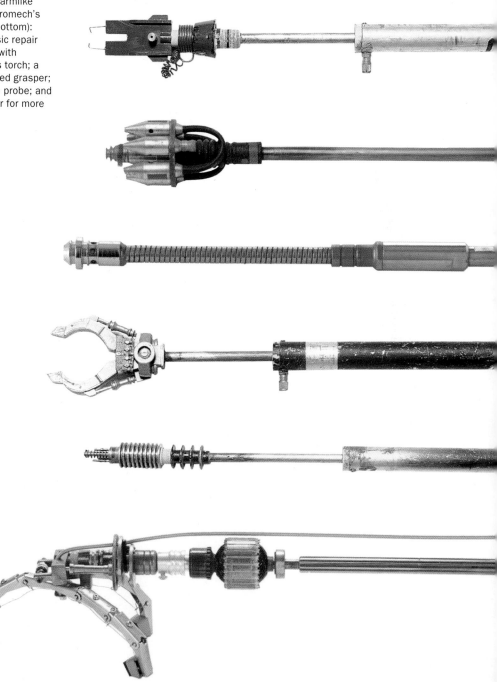

48

Staff of Power

Location: Endor
Date: 4 ABY

Compared to the hyperspace travelers of the Republic and the fortified presence of the Empire, the Ewoks, a tribe hailing from the Forest Moon orbiting the planet Endor, were often regarded as a primitive species. However, in 4 ABY, they not only aided the Rebel Alliance in its quest to take down a shield generator protecting the second Death Star, they also rid their forests of Imperial intruders who had set up a base on their world.

Each Ewok tribe was led by a chief, who relied on his experience and a number of special advisors to rule. Within their ranks were poets and storytellers who shared hard-won knowledge and deeply spiritual folklore. Star-watchers cared for the mystical wellbeing of the tribe and maintained peace with the spirits of the natural world, while the tribal shaman's understanding of native plants, ritual, and apparent magic made them noteworthy healers.

A staff of power like this once belonged to a tribal shaman called Logray. It is part of a collection of magical and medicinal items that helped him carry out his function among the clan. Sometimes called a spirit staff, elements of the design can easily be identified as a stick, some feathers, and a spine—scavenged from the forest floor or added to denote victory over an enemy. The staff was used in ceremonies to summon ancestral spirits, a ritual for calling on the dead to help the tribe in times of trouble. The staff complemented Logray's various other adornments, which included a headpiece fashioned from a churi bird skull and a ghost rattle. This was used in summoning spells or during the ritual sacrifice of outsiders.

Taken together, these artifacts tell us much about the Ewoks and their beliefs. They were adept warriors and trap makers, well able to use their vast knowledge of Endor to defeat those looking to turn their home into a war zone. Derived from natural resources, their technology efficiently defeated the Empire's supposedly sophisticated weaponry.

49

Boushh's Helmet

Location: Uba IV
Date: 4 ABY

Exiled from his homeworld of Uba IV, records of Boushh's familial identity and life on his planet were erased when he was cast out by his clan. Forced to wear his armor as a mark of shame, Boushh and a crew of four other outcasts roamed the galaxy in the days of the Empire. A skilled tracker renowned for sneaking up on targets undetected, Boushh soon made a formidable reputation as a bounty hunter.

On the world of Ord Mantell, however, Boushh met his match. During a shootout with the Rebels in an alleyway, Leia disarmed Boushh with her trusty blaster. With the help of R2-D2, Chewbacca, and Maz Kanata, the bounty hunter was rendered unconscious and stripped of his armor. Leia used Boushh's fatigues as a disguise—the Ubese's slender build and short stature perfectly suited the 1.5-meter- (5-foot-) tall Rebel. Leia realized it would take more than matching the bounty hunter's physique to con the scoundrels and low-lifes who knew Boushh best. Helping Lando Calrissian escape bounty hunters on the planet Arkanis gave her the chance to put her undercover abilities to the test. She then disguised herself in Boushh's armor to infiltrate the palace of Jabba the Hutt on Tatooine and rescue Han Solo from his cruel imprisonment in a block of carbonite.

Boushh's helmet is equipped with a vision-plus scanner; targeting laser; and refined auditory components, including a broadband antenna for receiving transmissions. It also has a metal speech scrambler where the mouth should be. This enabled Leia to address the Hutt in garbled Ubese.

Wearing the helmet and the rest of Boushh's outfit, even Leia's closest friends would have had difficulty identifying her, and she managed to fool Jabba. Unfortunately, when Leia sneaked into Jabba's throne room to free Han, she removed Boushh's headgear. Jabba and his entourage entered and she was quickly captured.

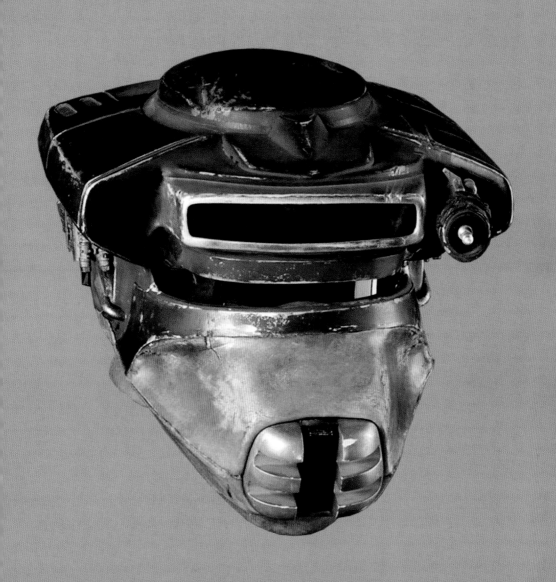

50

Han Solo's Dice

Location: *Millennium Falcon*
Date: 10 BBY

There were many variants of the rules governing the card game sabacc, long a favorite among gamblers and swindlers, but chance cubes were sometimes needed to generate random totals, as each player tried to maintain a hand with cards that added up to zero.

This particular pair of aurodium-plated chance cubes was a lucky charm for the smuggler Han Solo. He may even have used them in the game of sabacc that won him his prized freighter, the *Millennium Falcon*, from the professional gambler Lando Calrissian.

For years, the dice dangled from the cockpit ceiling of the YT-1300 freighter that long served as a symbol of hope, first for the Rebel Alliance and later for the Resistance. The dice certainly brought the courageous Han and his faithful copilot Chewbacca plenty of good fortune. With them at the controls, the *Falcon* helped the Rebellion turn the tide of the Battle of Yavin for a shock victory over Imperial forces that ended with the total destruction of the first Death Star.

Solo himself never revealed the precise significance of his lucky dice to anyone, but they were among his most prized possessions. The little golden cubes were the only item he owned that had once belonged to his father, Ovan. He once worked for the Corellian Engineering Corporation, building YT-1300s. His fervent wish was for his son to grow up to have a better life, flying across the galaxy instead of shackled to an assembly line. Sadly, young Han was snatched by the White Worms criminal clan and forced to do their bidding as a scrumrat.

Solo would probably never have admitted it at the time, but the dice were a comfort to him during the wretched years he spent in service to the White Worms. Although in later life Han generally despised sentimental souvenirs, the dice remained a powerful symbol for him—totems of his conviction that, with a little bit of luck, no odds were too great to overcome.

51

Mos Eisley Cantina Dispenser

Location: Tatooine
Date: 1 BBY

Politicians liked to believe that the most significant agreements and deals were made in the hallowed halls of the Galactic Senate. However, in the shadows of the Empire's monuments to its own grandeur, members of the underworld and the Rebellion made important pacts of their own while seated in the shadows of some of the seediest cantinas in any quadrant.

On the sun-soaked planet of Tatooine, Chalmun's Spaceport Cantina in Mos Eisley offered a welcome respite for weary travelers, freighter pilots awaiting their next job, and ne'er-do-wells looking for somewhere to lie low. The dimly lit interior was a great place to escape the heat, enjoy a drink, some live music, and relax.

A modest array of dispensers like this one—actually the hollowed-out head of an IG assassin droid repurposed for more pleasant purposes—could be spotted by the oblong bar. They allowed the bartender a clear sightline to the door for identifying potential troublemakers.

At more glamorous establishments, one might find a selection of Sullustan wines and small-batches of Toniray. This bright blue, sparkling concoction became a particularly rare delicacy for connoisseurs after Alderaan—where the fruits were grown—was destroyed by the Empire. At the rougher cantinas, taverns that required weapons to be checked at the door, it was common to find batches of pre-mixed beverages served in jugs and quick-access dispensers like this one.

Among the most popular beverages at the Mos Eisley cantina were the local staple of blue milk, as well as about a dozen drinks on tap. In towering silver dispensers were local concoctions like the Tatooine Sunset, Jawa Juice, and the Hutt's Delight, named for the crime boss Jabba of the Hutt Clan.

52

Enfys Nest's Helmet

Location: Savareen
Date: 10 BBY

There have been many factions in the history of the galaxy. Countless governments have gained power only to be toppled by competing interests, in a seemingly endless cycle of conflict. Ever-present amid the turmoil, pirates, thieves, and scoundrels of all kinds sought to build their own fiefdoms. Caring nothing for whichever side aspired to control the galaxy at the time, these rogues operated beyond the reach of any law, according to their own codes and values.

Despite a reputation as bloodthirsty marauders, Enfys Nest and the Cloud-Riders were largely misunderstood. Unlike the five main underworld crime syndicates, the Cloud-Riders mounted operations to survive rather than gain wealth or power. They were free spirits who instinctively opposed the Empire's draconian rule. Like many bounty hunters and mercenaries, Cloud-Riders hid their identity beneath a fearsome helmet, part of an ensemble that included a chest box vocoder that altered the wearer's voice for intimidation and camouflage.

This helmet was worn by teenager Enfys Nest, who had taken the mantle of Cloud-Rider leader. Fashioned from bone and metal, the helmet tells its own story of survival, perseverance, and triumph. An inscription along the top reads: "Until we reach the last edge, the last opening, the last star, and can go no higher." As well as protection, the helmet had another functional purpose: the antennae hidden in the bony protrusions on the top were vital for communications amongst the Cloud-Riders.

The circular symbol along the brow ridge that encompasses the chromed visor suggests that, at least from the point of view of the Cloud-Riders' leader, the group was operating with heroic intentions. The dark circle with the singular point of light at its center could symbolize a reverse eclipse, a literal light or a beacon surrounded by darkness.

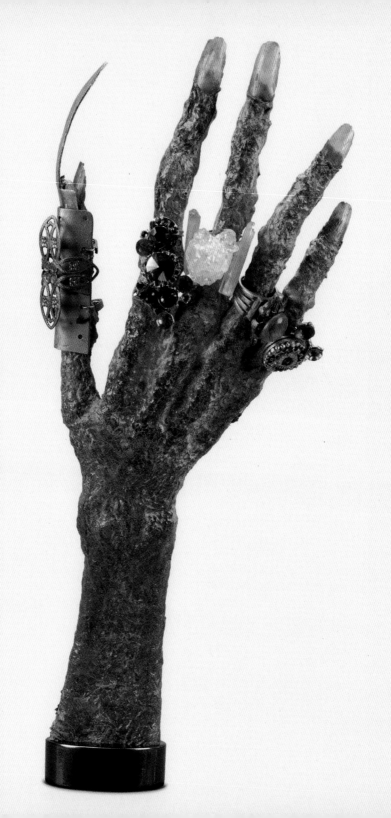

53

Hand of the Lost King of Duro

Collected by: Dryden Vos
Date: 10 BBY

This mummified hand belonged to the mysterious Lost King of Duro. The macabre artifact was one of the rare antiquities in the extensive collection of the underworld kingpin Dryden Vos. The wealthy leader of the Crimson Dawn crime syndicate was extremely proud of his museum-grade collection of strange treasures from across the galaxy. Among his most prized possessions was a near-complete set of Mandalorian armor dating back to the age of the Old Republic; rare animals preserved in suspended animation; and an ark allegedly containing the ashes of Chancellor Contispex I. Yet none of these are as bizarre as this single, shriveled hand.

The Duros are one of the oldest spacefaring species in the galaxy and their exploration efforts were essential to the foundation of the Galactic Republic. The Duros' royal line is as storied and important as the houses of Alderaan and Corellia in this long-lost era. Members of this humanoid species have a striking appearance: large red eyes, downturned mouths (often mistaken as indicative of disapproval), bulbous heads, and blue-green skin.

The coloration of the hand in Vos's collection has faded to a sickly brown owing to the preservation process, and the fingernails—now more like claws—are a sickly yellow hue. Yet, the status of the Lost King remains clear from the jewels that decorate each finger—clear evidence of the monarch's considerable wealth.

On the smallest digit is a locket holding the preserved biological material of the royal bloodline. This cell sample was a valuable means of proving the authenticity of the strange name given to this withered limb.

54

Han Solo's DL-44 Blaster

Location: Vandor
Date: 10 BBY

For some, war is profit. The titans behind BlasTech Industries know that better than most. The arms manufacturer has done a booming business for decades, supplying both sides during several galaxy-spanning conflicts with blaster pistols, rifles, and E-web cannons, among a steadily evolving roster of deadly weaponry.

Favored by the smuggler and Rebel Alliance general Han Solo, the DL-44 heavy blaster pistol remains a standout for its versatility in the field. Solo once declared that the power of the Force and a Jedi lightsaber were not half as useful as "a good blaster at your side." Solo was undoubtedly speaking of his trusty DL-44. This sidearm served him well for over 30 years, throughout the Galactic Civil War and into the early days of the First Order conflict.

A relic of Solo's days in the Imperial military, his first DL-44 blaster was a gift from his mentor, the gangster Tobias Beckett. Given Solo's dangerous line of work as a smuggler and later among the Rebels, it's impossible to know if Solo used a single DL-44 or, more likely, had several.

BlasTech's DL-44 model was renowned for condensing heavy firepower into a small, easily handled weapon. The blaster was also very adaptable. It could be reconfigured into a field rifle or stripped down to a pistol that could be carried at the hip. A Zoltwen D3x macroscope helped to increase the accuracy of this rugged firearm. Another notable feature, which could mean the difference between life and death in a shootout, was the low-power pulse warning in the handle.

During the era of the New Republic, technological advancements rendered the DL-44 model somewhat obsolete. But Solo, well aware of what worked for him, remained loyal to the blaster. The weapon was ever-present in his personal arsenal throughout his career until his untimely death.

55

Thermal Detonator

Location: Tatooine
Date: 4 ABY

A blast from thermal detonator can turn an enemy attack into a virtual suicide mission in seconds. In use for centuries during many wartime engagements, portability and tremendous destructive power combine in this tiny sphere.

With a volatile baradium plasma core concealed in a fragmentation shell, this handheld explosive is a last-resort battle tactic. When blaster fire is unable to bring victory, a thermal detonator may be employed to deliver a crushing blow and win the day.

However, using a thermal detonator carries a major risk. Once armed, the projectile gives its thrower just a few seconds to put a safe distance—between 5 and 15 meters (16 to 50 feet)—between themselves and the resulting blast. Many fighters failed to gain the necessary cover in time and were obliterated in the act of taking down their enemy.

These spherical grenades, compact enough to fit into the palm of the average hand, were regarded as a brutal weapon well suited to a savage, lawless world. The deadly devices were expensive to buy on the black market and criminals and bounty hunters developed a liking for them as an intimidating indication of wealth and power. Simply holding one at the ready, disarmed but fully functional, could be an effective power play. Just the flick of a thumb switch could completely turn the tide of a serious dispute.

In disguise as the bounty hunter Boushh, Leia Organa once employed a ploy such as this in a negotiation with the crime boss Jabba the Hutt. According to the files of the protocol droid C-3PO, Organa even armed the device to make her point, a truly courageous if incredibly dangerous move, to make it clear she wasn't joking. Luckily, this show of strength earned the Hutt's respect and entry into his innermost sanctum. There Leia was successful in freeing her love, Han Solo, from his carbonite prison. He had endured hanging on Jabba's wall for nearly a year.

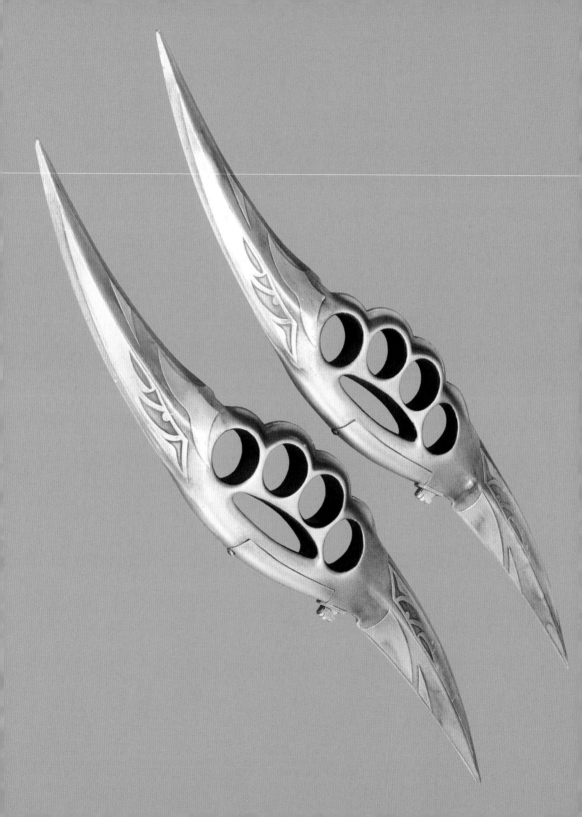

56

Dryden Vos's Petars

Location: *First Light*
Date: 10 BBY

Dryden Vos, one-time figurehead of the Crimson Dawn crime syndicate, was an intriguing individual. Traveling the galaxy on his yacht, the *First Light*, he stood out among other crime bosses for his fondness for antiquities and liking for finery. He showcased his syndicate's formidable wealth and his impeccable taste whenever he entertained his many affluent business contacts. Unlike some of his underworld competitors, Vos refused to allow success to make him careless and lackadaisical—prudent for a gangster who had made many enemies during his criminal career.

To defend himself if his security forces failed in their duty—or turned against him—Vos commissioned this pair of Kyuzo petars. A species known for its fast reflexes, the Kyuzo specialized in creating customized weaponry to meet an individual fighter's combat requirements.

Although often mistaken for someone of the human species, Vos's near-human nature was reflected in the knives' design, which, to fit his hands, included a hole for a sharpened thumb claw. Cast in bronzium, the petars were weighted to match Vos's particular combat style. He was a practitioner of Teräs Käsi, a martial art that consists of meditative postures and stances designed specifically for those at odds with Force-wielders. These maneuvers were also highly effective against those without Force-sensitivity, especially when Vos was wielding these blades.

Aside from their tempered carbon edges and filigree decoration—which endows the knives with a kind of fatal beauty—hidden power cells ignite monomolecular laser sheaths. Their energy field makes the knives even deadlier, turning their sharp edges into blades with cauterizing properties, similar to a lightsaber.

The fine detail and craftsmanship of the Kyuzo design is undeniably impressive—rather like Vos's own veneer of refinement. Beneath the facade of a gentleman entrepreneur beat the heart of a criminal who would stop at nothing to achieve power and influence. The gang leader could quickly turn violent, and was notorious for dealing with those who displeased him with a ruthless efficiency bordering on psychosis.

57

Training Remote

Location: Coruscant
Date: 22 BBY

Training remotes were a staple tool for Jedi looking to maintain mental acuity as well as physical sharpness. Among the simplest forms of droid tech, they have remained nearly unchanged for centuries, despite numerous advances in technology and warfare.

When not in use, a remote resembles a toy sphere or some forgotten ship part, discarded by a mechanic in a rush. Switch one on, however, and this gadget becomes a combination of sparring partner and teacher. With a tracking sensor and shock-ray emitter, the remote follows its subject, firing off harmless bolts that sting but rarely cause any real pain.

Remotes were vital to young, would-be Jedi's training. They helped them to hone their physical senses as well as attune them to the Force thrumming all around them. Classrooms of younglings would wield training sabers and practice combat forms as hovering remotes darted to and fro. Repulsorlifts lifted the remotes into the air, and bursts of compressed air enabled them to maneuver at speed and made them highly unpredictable in their movements.

When young users made a mistake, they were reproved by a puff of compressed air. For older students, a factory preset mode administered a mild electric shock. Remotes could be reset to a range of intensity levels for more advanced students.

Aged 19, Luke Skywalker was too old to begin lightsaber training by most Jedi standards. Thus a training remote was a vital aid in helping him to understand how the Force could be used to anticipate a blaster bolt.

Years later, Luke used a remote to get little Grogu hopping from rock to rock. General Leia Organa also used one with her Padawan Rey on a jungle obstacle course in the forests of Ajan Kloss. Some five decades after the fall of the Jedi, their tools were still employed to teach succeeding generations about the Force and its wonders.

58

Spice Container

Location: Daiyu
Date: 9 BBY

Just the push of a button on a pressurized spice canister releases a puff of mind-altering spice into the air. For thousands of years this intoxicating escape from reality has proved irresistible to individuals all over the galaxy. Unrefined spice can be used for medicinal purposes, but the rainbow-hued drug is more often found on the black market. Spice is dealt on the streets and bartered for credits and other valuables.

The canisters sold in the Daiyu marketplace are a status symbol among spice users. Delicate vessels of glass and copper-plated numinal, they are small enough to fit in the palm of one's hand. Their intricate design is calculated to appeal to a traveler with the time to relax and enjoy their spice-induced state.

The illicit spice trade fuels much of the economy of the criminal underworld. Its dark history can be traced to the Outer Rim world of Kessel, In the days of the Empire, courts sometimes sentenced criminals to work in the planet's infamous mines. Miners were also abducted from their home worlds without justification. The Wookiees of Kashyyyk made up an inordinately high number of Kessel miners at one time; no records can be found that they committed any crimes. The Wookiee race did not forget or forgive its exploitation and treatment by the Empire.

The mines were managed by the Pyke Syndicate. The prisoners and enslaved who made up the workforce often died there. Some were crushed by faulty machinery, others died from sheer exhaustion. A few succumbed to accidental overdose after breathing in too much spice in air lacking proper filtration equipment.

While the Empire fabricated reasons to incarcerate powerful Wookiees to mine the stuff, it also turned a blind eye to the spice trade. In the bustling dens on planets like Daiyu, free samples were openly handed out on the streets to unsuspecting travelers. Pushers gave the first hit away for free, often from a spice stick, confident in the drug's addictive qualities to create a new clientele who would soon be in need of a canister of their own.

59

Max Rebo's Red Ball Jett Organ

Location: Tatooine
Date: 4 ABY

In the waning years of Jabba the Hutt's grip as the Daimyo of Tatooine, the Ortolan musician Max Rebo and his red ball jett organ were the mainstay of the house band at Jabba's Palace. Rebo was the bandleader for a roster that could number up to a dozen players, singers, and dancers. The percussive rhythm of the red ball jett helped the Max Rebo Band keep the beat.

At 1.4 meters (4 feet 6 inches) in diameter, the organ is somewhat unwieldy. It is also fragile, so more suited to musicians playing residencies than those traveling from gig to gig. An air intake and a speaker is located on the sides of the instrument. The front is ringed by 21 keys corresponding to pipes built into the frame. The player summons notes by pressing the keys, which release air through valves at the base of the instrument. The entire kit is held together by a metal girdle. This adds to the instrument's aesthetic appeal, and prevents sound vibrations from warping the outer shell. The red ball jett was capable of storing tracks and recording sound. For Rebo, that meant he could jam with himself live, playing along with a prerecorded backing track.

Ortolan musicians have the perfect physique for playing the instrument. The considerable reach of these blue-skinned aliens' two, 10-toed limbs is ideal for covering the keys, while their buttocks comfortably perch on the cushion at the center. Beings with more limbs have tried to become proficient players, but with mixed results. Taller species have modified the organ so that they can stand at the center of the instrument.

During sets, Max Rebo liked to snack on salty delicacies, such as cured ronto sticks, and so his red ball jett organ had a special food compartment. His insatiable appetite even resulted in him agreeing to play at Jabba's Palace in exchange for free meals.

This musical instrument is one of the oldest in the galaxy. Versions of it have been found in ancient temples and the sonorous melody of the jett's pipes may be heard in some of the galaxy's oldest songs.

60

Rebel Manifesto

Location: Aldhani
Date: 5 BBY

Saw Gerrera is often considered the first leader of the Rebel cause. Before the fall of the Republic, this violent Onderonian extremist rose up against his homeworld's government, who had joined the Separatist faction. Yet he was not the true architect of the Rebel Alliance, which involved unifying many factions fighting for the same goal under one banner.

That position may be said to belong to a young idealist named Karis Nemik who, in the pages of what would effectively become the Rebel manifesto, set down his thoughts on the oppressive Imperial machine. It remains one of the precious few documents that guided and helped to motivate scattered rebel cells during the early days of the Alliance.

"The pace of oppression outstrips our ability to understand it," Nemik wrote. "That is the real trick of the Imperial thought machine." The manifesto is effectively a blueprint for dismantling Palpatine's Empire.

After making the acquaintance of a mysterious mercenary named Clem, Nemik came to believe that hired guns might play an important part in a plot to overthrow the Emperor. "Weapons are tools; those that use them are by extension functional assets that we must use to our best advantage," he wrote. "The Empire has no moral boundaries. Why should we not take hold of every chance we can? Let them see how an insurgency adapts."

Sometimes referred to as *The Trail of Political Consciousness*, Nemik's untitled work exemplifies the intellectual climate that fostered the Rebel revolt to restore democracy. The manifesto espoused freedom, independence, and justice. It is also credited with helping to inspire Cassian Andor to join the growing unrest. Without Nemik's writings, Andor might never have gone on to work on the frontlines of the turmoil. He became a crucial member of Rebel intelligence, an adept spy dedicated to the Alliance and willing to sacrifice his life for freedom.

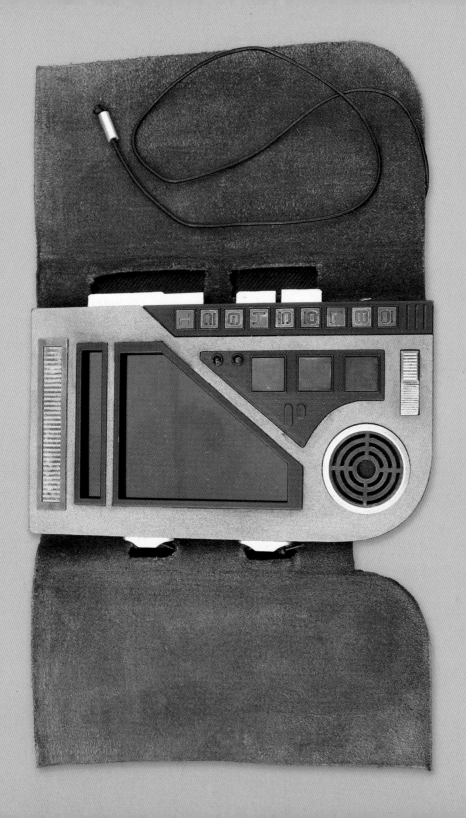

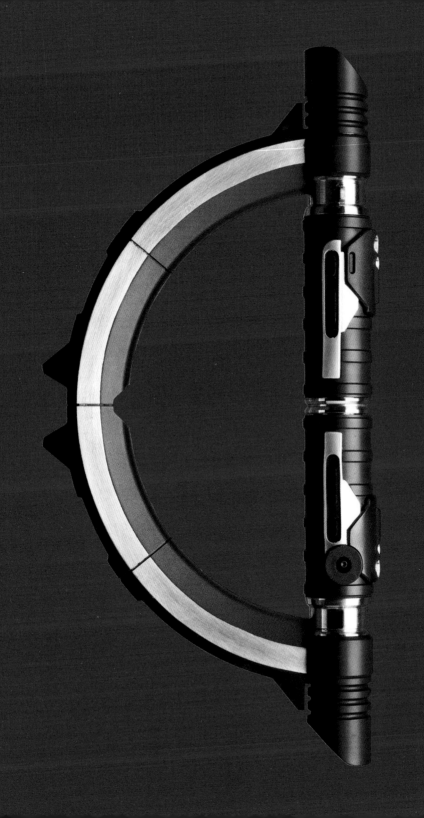

61
Reva's Lightsaber

Location: Nur
Date: 9 BBY

Order 66 brought a swift and brutal end to the Jedi Order. However, there were those Jedi who evaded the slaughter and lived to fight another day. Around the year 19 BBY the Inquisitorius was formed by the Empire to hunt down and eliminate these scattered Jedi and other Force-sensitive beings. The Inquisitors' headquarters was in a fortress in the ocean depths of the watery moon of Nur. Most responded to a number combined with a familial reference. This lightsaber belonged to the Third Sister. She proved to be an outlier in the program for her unique blade, her aspirations to become Grand Inquisitor, and her personal agenda.

In the days of the Republic, the Third Sister was a Jedi youngling who answered to the name Reva and studied at the Jedi Temple on Coruscant. Reva watched in horror as her classmates and friends were cut down by the blade of Darth Vader, the fallen Jedi she had known as Anakin Skywalker.

On the surface, it would appear that Reva followed in his sinister footsteps. She allied herself with the dark side and served Vader as a Jedi hunter. As the Third Sister, she carried a glowing, dual-bladed red lightsaber with a circular guard on the hilt. This was standard equipment for the Inquisitors, similar to the Grand Inquisitor's own blade. Reva's weapon was different, however. She could split it in two, so that a cumbersome 2-meter (6-foot-6-inch) saber could become two swords.

Reva's saber reflected her dual motivations, which set her apart from her brothers and sisters of the darkness. The other Inquisitors were dedicated to the dark side, the hierarchy, and the Empire—a perversion of the Jedi's dedication to the light, their own masters, and the Republic—and some were corrupted Jedi like Skywalker. Reva had her own reasons for joining the Inquisitorius. She had witnessed the brutal end of the Jedi Order with her own eyes, surviving only by feigning death and hiding among the corpses of the fallen. When she joined the Empire, she had no intention of blindly serving Darth Vader. Instead, Reva hoped to catch the Sith Lord off guard and, with her twin blades, exact instant vengeance for the only family she had ever known.

62

Sky Kyber Pendant

Location: Coruscant
Date: 5 BBY

Among collectors of jewels and antiquities, this sky kyber pendant is highly regarded for its two-toned crystal, as well as the historical conflict it has come to symbolize.

Hanging from a 42-centimeter (16-and-a-half-inch) chain, the pendant boasts a cerulean stone that culminates in the clear white of a pure kyber crystal, a rare variation of the kyber gems found throughout the galaxy. At the time of the Empire's reign, an item such as this could fetch anything from 30,000 to 50,000 credits on the open market. A bidding war might increase the value well beyond these estimates.

The necklace commemorates the uprising of the Kuati people against the humanoid amphibious Rakatans who had invaded their world. It was once the property of Luthen Rael, a prominent antiques dealer on Coruscant's upper levels.

To the discerning eye, aware of the crystal's history, the sky kyber pendant is much more than just another valuable jewel. It is a physical reminder of the natural order of things. Like the Rebel Alliance that arose to unseat the tyrannical Imperial regime, the Kuati took great pride in self-governance and democracy before the Rakatans overran their planet. Through the Kuati's rebellion, balance and order was restored, a state reflected in the meeting of the pendant's sky blue crystal with its pure white counterpart.

On a spiritual level, the unusually colored pendant is a reminder of the days of the Jedi Order when kyber crystals were used to help the knights of old power their lightsabers and aid the defenseless. With the Jedi virtually eradicated during the Empire's reign, kyber crystals remained a crucial symbol of the Force itself.

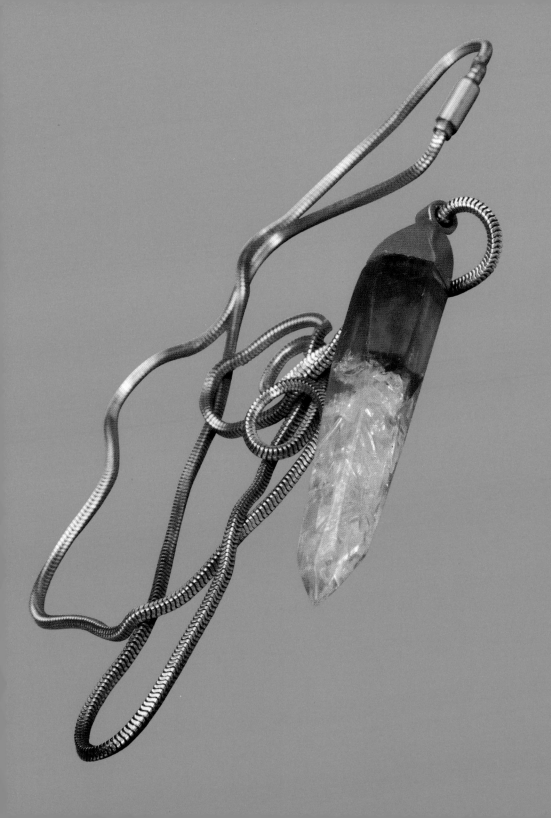

63

X-Wing Pilot Helmet

Location: D'Qar
Date: 34 ABY

For decades, the Rebels looked to the Imperial Navy and then to the pilots of the New Republic to supply skilled fliers to crew their fleets. By recruiting capable cadets from within official facilities, Rebel forces gained the advantages of, in some cases, years of combat training, as well as a deeper understanding of enemy tactics. Trading Imperial fatigues for revolutionary garb was life-changing for these recruits in more ways than one. Compared to the immaculate TIE fighter pilot helmets of the Empire, polished to a shine, a Rebel X-wing or Y-wing pilot's helmet looked like something pulled from a trash compactor. But looks can be deceiving.

Luke Skywalker dreamed of leaving his home on Tatooine and joining his friends Biggs and Tank as a cadet at the Imperial Academy. Although he had no love for the Empire, like his father Anakin he had a gift for deft piloting and longed for the freedom seemingly offered by the Imperial training.

In the year 0 ABY, Luke joined the Rebel Alliance, and was a key member of the Red Squadron that flew in the Battle of Yavin. Wearing this helmet, he fired the one-in-a-million shot that hit the Death Star at its weakest point and destroyed the Empire's ultimate superweapon .

Skywalker was still wearing the helmet when he flew his X-wing to Ahch-To in the year 28 ABY, intending to live out his days in exile. He abandoned his craft, allowing it to sink to the bottom of the sea. Recovered by Luke's Force ghost, the helmet was worn by the Jedi Knight Rey Skywalker during the Resistance's last stand at the Battle of Exegol. Donning it was her way of paying homage to the freedom fighters of the previous generation who had sacrificed so much to restore a true Republic.

The bulkier construction of older model helmets like Luke Skywalker's did not necessarily equate to greater protection. Some recruits were honored to wear them. Others either had to wear old gear or go without. Pilots quickly learned not to complain, recognizing that the Rebellion had to make do with

patched-together ships and other outdated technology to get by.

In her youth, the scavenger Rey recovered the helmet of the fallen Captain Dosmit Ræh of the Tierfon Yellow Aces from the graveyard of the Battle of Jakku. It became a treasured possession. In her converted AT-AT dwelling late at night, Rey would put on the helmet, look up at the stars, and imagine the freedom of flight.

Although the design of an X-wing helmet was standard for most humanoid species, decorations and symbols were unique to each pilot. These included their squadron insignia as well as other personal touches. The center ridge contained reinforced interior padding and plating that cradled the skull. Headsets and microphones were implanted inside each helmet for communication with other pilots, ground crews, and commanders. Some pilots used the blank spaces on the their helmets to mark their victories. Others used them to express their own artistic creativity or affix a memento from their loved ones.

In the first days of the conflict against the First Order, Rebel pilots able to benefit from the initial influx of funds that helped General Leia Organa organize the Resistance managed to acquire newer helmets. Among those early recruits, the pilot Poe Dameron benefitted from a more streamlined one, with a slim silhouette and custom fit. Painted black to reflect his status as the leader of Black Squadron, the sides bore the red insignia of the Resistance, the same starbird once worn by Rebel Alliance fighters in numerous battles.

Other Resistance members, including Nien Nunb, a Sullustan pilot, and the Abednedo Ello Asty were equipped with customized helmets. Gazing upon a row of X-wing pilot helmets, one can imagine the faces that peered out from behind the visors over the years. Their helmets' scruffy beauty is a testament to the Rebels' indomitable spirit.

Opposite page: At the start of the Galactic Civil War, these 12 helmets were worn by Rebel fighters stationed at the secret base on Yavin 4. They belonged to (top to bottom, left to right): Derek Klivian, Red Squadron; Attico Wred, Green Squadron; Ralo Surrel, Red Squadron; Barion Raner, Blue Squadron; Jon Vander, leader of Gold Squadron; Broan Danurs, Green Squadron; Wion Dillems, Green Squadron; Riss Clyos, Green Squadron; Datchi Creel, Gold Squadron; Torge Sommer, Green Squadron; Torius Chord, Blue Squadron; and Zal Dinnes, Red Squadron.

During the age of the Resistance, X-wing pilot Poe Dameron wore this customized helmet.

64

Landspeeder

Location: Tatooine
Date: 0 ABY

Originally produced by the SoroSuub Corporation, an X-34 landspeeder was one of young Luke Skywalker's most treasured possessions. It was acquired second or third hand for 2,400 credits when Skywalker was a teen living on the Lars homestead. The craft was ideal for running errands around the moisture farm and tending to vaporator maintenance. It was also Skywalker's main means of escaping from his chores to meet friends in Anchorhead or cruise among the dunes. Unlike his T-16 skyhopper, the

landspeeder was limited to local travel, being built to hover only about a meter (3 feet 4 inches) above the ground. Although the speeder gave Luke the feeling of freedom, the machine's limitations ensured that he remained tethered safely to his home patch.

Measuring 3.4 meters (11 feet) in length, the craft could reach speeds of up to 250 kph (155 mph), gliding over the sands with ease. The harsh climate of Tatooine bleached the vibrant red paint of Skywalker's speeder. Sand kicked up as the vehicle accelerated scrubbed the front down to the bare metal and sandstorms left much of its bodywork pocked and dented.

For Luke, his landspeeder was a pet project. He put a considerable amount of time and credits into maintaining the vehicle's repulsorlifts and tinkering under the hood to coax optimal performance from its engines. He cared little about its beat-up appearance; perhaps he even relished the fact that, despite its shabby looks, his speeder packed a genuinely powerful punch.

In prime working order, the trio of air-cooled turbines, combined with a reclaimed antigravity generator, provided a surprisingly smooth and comfortable ride for up to two beings. Over the dorsal exhaust vents there was sufficient space for a droid or to store cargo that did not need the protection of the speeder's duraplex windshield.

X-34 models like this one, once owned by Luke Skywalker, were considered outdated by 0 ABY, when XP-38 models dominated the industry.

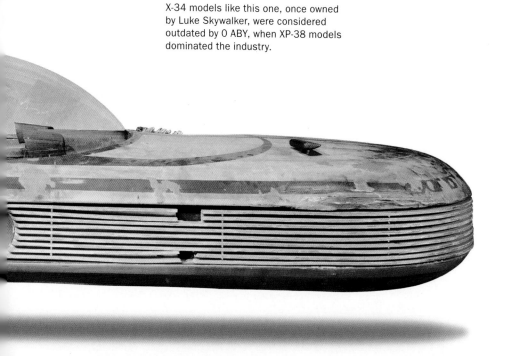

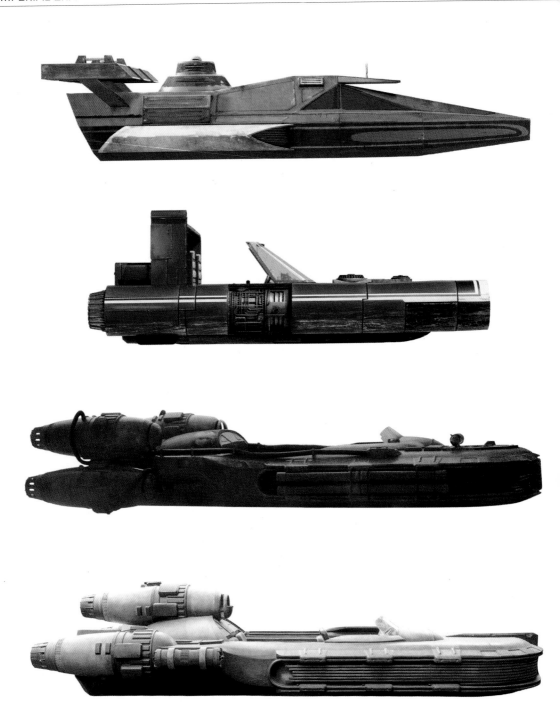

Luke did not just inherit his father Anakin's remarkable mechanical aptitude and Force sensitivity, he also possessed his restlessness. This trait gave him a love of speed for its own sake and made it difficult for him to remain in one place for long.

The landspeeder took a fair few hits as young Luke raced his friends for bragging rights through the canyons around his home. On the front end alone, a womp-rat-size dent indicated an unlucky encounter with one of Tatooine's native species.

Luke's landspeeder's rather lopsided appearance could have been caused by him removing the cowling on the left thrust turbine after some converter coil wires burned out. This would have allowed air to flow naturally over the turbine to prevent it overheating. A full repair would have required Luke to make a trip to Tosche Station to pick up a new or refurbished regulator.

One fateful day, Luke was at the landspeeder's controls when he pulled into the Lars homestead. A terrible sight greeted him. Unbeknownst to Luke, the Empire was hunting for him and had traced a pair of recently purchased droids, R2-D2 and C-3PO, back to his home. A squad of stormtroopers, secretly dispatched to find Luke, had murdered his uncle Owen and aunt Beru and burned the family farm to the ground to cover their tracks. The mission was officially logged as a dispute among locals and conveniently blamed upon the Tusken Raiders native to that harsh desert world.

Luke had been eager to escape Tatooine and the mundane life of a moisture farmer even before this traumatic, tragic discovery. This was despite the fervent protestations of his foster family, who had cared for him since he was a baby. Now, with the only home he had ever known in smoldering ruins and his adoptive parents dead, there was nothing to keep him tethered to the Lars smallholding.

In the year 0 ABY, Skywalker sold his beloved landspeeder for 2,000 credits at a sleazy, used-speeder dealership operating in Mos Eisley. The credits from the sale went to pay the pilot Han Solo, and Luke, along with the Jedi Master Obi-Wan Kenobi, and the droids R2-D2 and C-3PO, booked passage to Alderaan.

Opposite page: The look of landspeeder models varied from the V-35 (top), designed as a courier vehicle, to the Mobquet M-68, (second from top), a favorite among Corellian racing enthusiasts. Most models (for example, the bottom two examples), retained the same basic details for generations.

New Republic Era

The Rebellion's success at the Battle of Jakku heralds a new dawn, but peace is not so easily restored from the ashes of the Empire.

Imperial remnants are adrift from their former grandeur, yet still power-hungry and heavily armed. In the absence of democracy, the underworld has prospered. A web of gangsters and bounty hunters seek their own fiefdoms to rule over, free from the laws of the Empire or the freshly established New Republic. On Nevarro, the Bounty Hunters Guild enforces its own code; on Tatooine, crime lords vie for control of the Hutts' criminal empire.

In the greater galaxy, the government, led by Mon Mothma with Senator Leia Organa among its representatives, grapples with a new identity. Meanwhile, the last Jedi, Luke Skywalker, begins teaching the next generation of Force users, erecting a school on Ossus to pass on what he has learned.

65

Boba Fett's Z-6 Jetpack

Location: Tatooine
Date: 4 ABY

Whether facing down small starfighters, other warriors, or even Force-sensitive combatants, a jetpack was a means of gaining the upper hand. Boba Fett's jetpack's primary function was to provide him with the ability to fly. It was also often equipped with a top-loaded homing missile for hitting long-range targets. The device was modeled after similar packs favored by Mandalorians for generations. Once vibrantly painted in sky blue and golden yellow with red and silver accents, the paint had faded from years of use.

The jetpack was badly damaged during the Rebel rescue to free Han Solo from his carbonite prison, ensconced on the wall of Jabba the Hutt's Palace. As a result, the pack malfunctioned, sending Fett sailing into the side of Hutt's sail barge *Khetanna* and then into the gaping maw of a Sarlacc in the Great Pit of Carkoon. For a time, many believed Boba Fett to be dead.

After clawing his way back to the surface, having barely survived being digested by the beast, Boba was discovered unconscious by a band of Jawa scavengers and stripped of his armor, jetpack, and identity. He was then taken captive by a tribe of Tusken Raiders. Fett found new purpose at the Tusken camp and was eventually accepted as one of the tribe after earning their respect.

Fett's equipment was salvaged by a man called Cobb Vanth, who used his intimidating helmet, armor, and Z-6 jetpack to keep the peace in the small town of Mos Pelgo, later known as Freetown. The jetpack later briefly passed into the hands of the Mandalorian Din Djarin. Fett was finally reunited with his jetpack and the rest of his armor in 9 ABY.

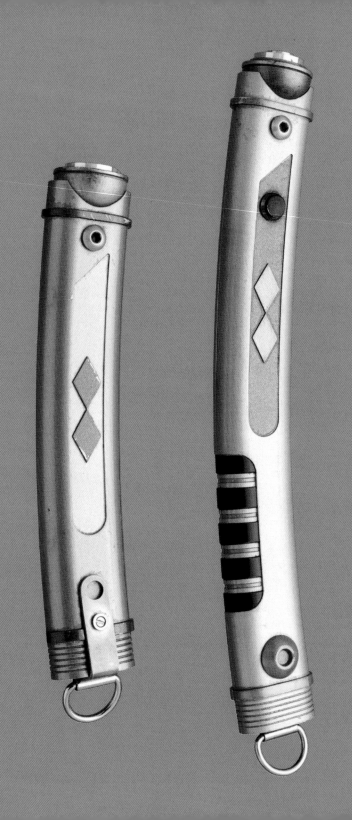

66

Ahsoka Tano's Lightsabers

Location: Corvus
Date: 9 BBY

An ancient Jedi proverb states: "Your lightsaber is your life." For the Force-wielders who found their ilk thrust into the crucible of the Clone Wars, this adage became extremely pertinent. It was not uncommon for a Jedi to lose their weapons over the course of their lives, rebuilding new hilts and securing new kyber crystals to power them. Building a new blade signaled a turning point in a Jedi's life. In the case of an individual who had been lost to the Order, it could signify that they had embarked upon a very different path.

Ahsoka Tano was apprenticed to Anakin Skywalker at the age of 14, learning from the troubled young Jedi Knight in the early days of the Clone Wars. At 16, Tano returned to the ice planet Ilum to obtain a second kyber crystal. Although she retained her first saber, Ahsoka also built a shoto lightsaber with a shorter blade and began learning the art of Jar'Kai combat. Tano abandoned these lightsabers after she witnessed the implementation of the Empire's Order 66, when the clone troopers she had fought alongside became mindless drones bent on destroying the Jedi.

Like most Jedi survivors, cut off from the life she had known, Tano went into hiding. It is believed that early in the time of the Empire's reign, Ahsoka had a vision in which she built a new set of lightsabers. Some claim these sabers were forged in conflict, like Tano herself, possibly trophies from the defeat of an Inquisitor hunting Tano. If they once glowed crimson in the hands of the Inquisitorius, Tano must have healed them and fashioned new, curved hilts, which still served her in the age of the New Republic. When ignited, their blades glowed a brilliant white, indicating that the crystals had been restored to their purest form.

67

Tracking Fob

Location: Nevarro
Date: 9 ABY

Those operating above the law and behind a veil of secrecy go to great lengths to conceal their identities. Disguises, carefully plotted routes away from major starports and, in the most drastic cases, facial reconstruction, aid those individuals in their surreptitious dealings. At the dawn of the Empire, the new regime attempted to clamp down on these activities. It did so through a program that required the mass registration of galactic citizens according to a numerical identification system known as a chain code.

Chain codes were used to record the movements of all who submitted to government surveillance, whether willingly or under duress. Tied to biometric data and biographical intel such as family history, the codes provided a snapshot of an individual's whole life. In the early days, these codes were challenging, but not impossible, to forge, but this was made more difficult with the passage of time. After the Empire was toppled and the New Republic reinstated, chain codes persisted as a means of identifying citizens.

By then, bounty hunters had learned how to utilize the codes to locate and identify victims with the assistance of tracking fobs. These were handed out to members of the Bounty Hunters Guild on Nevarro along with bounty pucks—rugged, compact holoprojectors that contained data on targets and the values placed on their heads.

It took an experienced hunter capable of networking for information and stalking prey to fully utilize a tracking fob. Linked to the chain code of its intended target, the short-range sensor antenna had to be brought quite close to the fugitive before it could locate the chain code signal. When it did so, it emitted a series of beeps and activated a red light wired into the casing.

Around 9 ABY, a galactic recession led to exceptionally low bounties, making the dangerous profession less attractive. As a result, at the request of the client ordering the bounty or at the discretion of the local Guild boss, high-value targets might be assigned to several bounty hunters equipped with identical tracking fobs. With bounty hunter competing against bounty hunter for the prize, their quarry had little chance of escape.

68

Beskar Ingots

Location: Nevarro
Date: 9 ABY

For generations, the warriors of Mandalore wore armor made from beskar, a metal alloy capable of deflecting blaster fire and even lightsaber blades. Although prominently utilized during the Mandalorian conflict with the Jedi Order, beskar's prevalence predates that ancient war and long outlasted the tension between the people of Mandalore and the Force users.

During the Siege of Mandalore in the waning days of the Clone Wars, the former Jedi Ahsoka Tano joined with the heir to the Mandalorian throne, Bo-Katan Kryze, to free the world from its dictatorial usurper, Maul. However, a new enemy soon arrived to dominate the citizens of Mandalore— the Empire. For a time, the clans successfully resisted Imperial occupation, led by Kryze, who wielded the legendary Darksaber. After she was unseated and Mandalore was laid to waste, she was blamed for accepting the throne without earning the right in battle. The story of the Lady Kryze became a cautionary tale told to children.

In what came to be known among the survivors—mostly descendants of the cloistered Death Watch, who lived on the moon of Concordia—as the Night of a Thousand Tears, the Empire destroyed Mandalore. Beskar armor was no defense against the bombardment. Imperials named the attack the Great Purge, using the genocide of an entire people to deter unrest on other worlds.

Beskar ingots are rare, but could still be found in the days of the New Republic, evidence of the Empire's past dominance. Mandalorian beskar was melted down into blocks stamped with the Imperial crest. Although the Empire enjoyed gloating about its domination of Mandalore and marking its most precious metal as its own, there is no evidence of Imperials utilizing beskar for armor. It is possible that the Empire had difficulty finding an armorer capable of shaping the metal into its strongest form.

After the Empire's reign ended, some ingots made their way into Mandalorian hands and were made into gleaming new armor by the few remaining artisans. Dating back to a time of Mandalorian prosperity, these armorers were revered and kept their knowledge closely guarded. For them, creating beskar armor was essentially an act of worship.

69

Amban Sniper Rifle

Location: Nevarro
Date: 9 ABY

This crude but highly effective firearm was well suited to bounty hunters operating in lawless underworlds. Manufactured by the Amban Arms Corporation the rifle is considered to be the source of several accounts that claim that Mandalorian arsenals routinely contained weaponry capable of disintegrating enemies on sight.

Topped with a removable electroscope for precise aim, the sniper rifle is tipped with a forked ion-prod electro-bayonet that was capable of turning an organic target to dust with a single squeeze of the trigger. On its highest setting, one blast would send a ionic pulse reverberating through a lifeform's essential systems. Contact with living matter vibrated the molecules so violently that the jolt and subsequent burst of released energy tore the target to shreds. A shower of sparks, charred flesh, and shreds of clothing were frequently all that was left, making victim-identification extremely difficult. For this reason, bounty hunters only used the rifle's highest setting as a last resort when hunting fugitives, as they could not claim success without at least the trophy of the intact head of their prey.

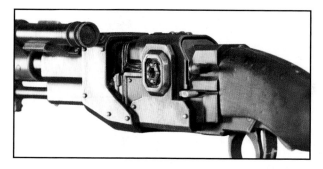

With the carry strap removed, the power-cell port hatch control is clearly visible. Amban rifles of this type are charged by Notimo-6 power cells. A new power cell is required for each high-powered disruptor round.

Weighing just 3.65 kilograms (8 lbs) and with a reinforced stock, the Amban rifle can also be used as a melee weapon. The firearm is calibrated to fire a shock of anywhere from 50,000 to 500,000 volts. If the two prongs are pressed into the flesh of an opponent they deliver a jolt that will incapacitate most species. Used against more massive creatures, this stun feature is little more than a painful annoyance, like a sudden pinching sensation.

In 9 ABY, the Mandalorian bounty hunter Din Djarin utilized his rifle's useful shock function to ward off a ravinak that threatened to consume his ship. He also used it to escape a krayt dragon that was terrorizing the community of the town of Mos Pelgo on Tatooine. In both cases, Djarin survived and neither creature was harmed.

70

Kuiil's Workbench

Location: Arvala-7
Date: 9 ABY

The Ugnaught Kuiil was once forced to toil in the Imperial gene farms, enslaved by the Empire, to pay off a debt incurred by his clan. For many years, he dreamed of a life of his own choosing. At last, after the fall of the Empire, he made his home as a free man on a vaporator farm in a dry gulch among the dust clouds and mud flats of Arvala-7.

A farmer putting down roots on a frontier planet must be resourceful by nature or quickly learn to be so in order to survive. Kuiil's workbench was built into the remnants of a discarded TIE fighter cockpit. He could look out over his valley through the reclaimed transparisteel windowframe. After dark, high-powered lights illuminated his workspace as he labored long into the night. Using various tools, Kuiil was extremely adept at retrofitting discarded parts and motors to fashion all kinds of machines.

Kuiil's creations could be found all around his farm, but there was no greater testament to his brilliance with a hydrospanner than his recovery of the fallen assassin droid IG-11. Kuiil recovered the IG unit's hardware from a compound abandoned by a band of mercenaries who had brought disorder and violence to his peaceful valley. He succeeded in reconstructing the droid over the course of many patient hours at his workbench. With just fragments of its neural harness remaining, he reprogrammed its primary functions, effectively teaching the droid to perform useful tasks on his farm. The droid's duties included feeding Kuiil's blurrgs and tending to routine chores, such as keeping the vaporators running efficiently. In time, IG-11 became a companion Kuiil could genuinely trust.

By all accounts, Kuiil was happiest at his workbench. With his goggles strapped to his stern-looking face, sparks flying as he worked out a complex mechanical problem, he found deep satisfaction in devising yet another quirky, labor-saving contraption.

71

Razor Crest Control Knob

Location: Tython
Date: 9 ABY

The foundling Grogu, a Force-sensitive child of the same species as Yoda, was about 50 standard years old when he was taken in by the Mandalorian bounty hunter Din Djarin. Grogu and Djarin formed their own clan of two, marked by the signet of a mudhorn. For a time, these unlikely allies traveled the galaxy, hiding from Imperial remnants who sought young Grogu for scientific experimentation. They lived aboard Djarin's refurbished *Razor Crest*, a retired military transport large enough to house his impressive arsenal of bounty-hunting tools.

Unscrewed from one of the levers in the cockpit of Djarin's beloved ship, at first glance this control knob bears a striking resemblance to a cybernetic eye. Grogu was entranced by it. Maybe it reminded him of some distant moon in the night sky or was simply a token of his found family and their home. Perhaps he just enjoyed the way the light glinted off its polished metal. Attached to a control lever, the knob itself may have seemed to possess a mysterious ability to transport them to their next adventure.

The control knob was one of the very few pieces of the vessel that remained intact following a direct hit from Moff Gideon's light cruiser. The blast decimated the *Razor Crest* on Tython and the foundling was kidnapped by Gideon's Dark Troopers. Fortunately, Djarin and Grogu were not separated for long. Grogu was rescued from imprisonment and returned to his training—nearly three decades after it was interrupted by the execution of Order 66. This time, his Master was one of the few remaining Jedi Knights: Luke Skywalker.

The Mudhorn clan was finally reunited on the arid world of Tatooine. To mark this happy occasion, Djarin gifted little Grogu the knob, which became a treasured heirloom for the brave child.

The distinctive top of Boba Fett's gaderffii stick.

72

Tusken Gaderffii Stick

Location: Tatooine
Date: 0 ABY

The Tusken Raiders, indigenous beings of the sand-covered world of Tatooine, have often been misrepresented and misunderstood. Tales shared by settlers at the local cantinas characterize the so-called "Sand People" as little more than roving clans of ruthless, bloodthirsty mercenaries. It is common for poor moisture farmers to invest in security sensors out of fear for their own safety, especially after dark.

While there are undoubtedly those among the Tusken tribes who live by violence, kidnapping, killing, or enslaving settlers, many Tuskens seek only a peaceful existence. Hidden away in the wilderness, these warriors of the Dune Sea are in touch with their world and maintain a strong spiritual connection with their ancestors and community.

Outsiders who spend time among the Tuskens portray them as fiercely loyal to their own and determined to defend their land against intruders. In many cases the strangers that live among certain tribes have been rescued from the desert and would have died if the Tuskens had not taken them in, providing food and water in exchange for their labor.

The Tusken gaderffii stick is an accurate representation of their culture and history, functioning both as a weapon and a tool. It also symbolizes an individual's spiritual journey to become a full-fledged member of the tribe. It is a rite of passage for young Tuskens to embark upon a spiritual quest, guided by a tiny gekko. This lizard exists symbiotically for a time, attached to the brain of the one seeking existential transformation. The Tuskens believe that, with the help of this creature, hallucinatory visions will expand understanding of the novitiate's place in the world, and lead them to the ancient wortwood tree, from which all gaderffii sticks are made.

There is some debate on the gekko's role in this ritual. Some believe it induces the hallucinatory state through its physical connection, traveling up the nose of the young Tusken and attaching itself to the central nervous

Left to right: melee weapons belonging
to two different warriors; a longer staff
denoting a clan leader's prominence;
Boba Fett's training stick.

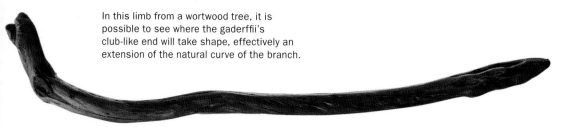

In this limb from a wortwood tree, it is possible to see where the gaderffii's club-like end will take shape, effectively an extension of the natural curve of the branch.

system. After helping to induce a meditative trance, the creature makes a painless exit that leaves the subject unharmed. Others suspect that a heavy dose of the drug spice is a more likely explanation for the visions.

Those who successfully complete the rite claim a branch from the tree and return to their settlements victorious and ready to begin crafting the raw wood into a gaderffii, or gaffi stick. Crafting a gaffi stick takes long hours of chiseling, chipping, and sanding to create the rounded knob at the top. When wielded as a club, with the right amount of force behind it, the stick is strong enough to shatter metal. This part of the gaffi often ends in a point that is forged in a special smelter to harden it. The point is a useful tool with a variety of uses. The Tuskens even use it to clean their banthas' teeth.

On the other end of the gaffi is a metal tip, forged from debris left behind by offworlders. This is sharp and strong enough to penetrate stormtrooper armor, puncturing the vital organs beneath the chest plate to swiftly kill. Measuring about 1.3 meters (4 feet 4 inches) long, each gaderffii is unique, a reflection of its owner and one of their most precious possessions. Those who lose their gaffi stick or see it destroyed in combat are made to repeat the ritual or risk being cast out from their clan.

During the years of his transformation from bounty hunter to Daimyo of Tatooine, Boba Fett was welcomed into a tribe of Tuskens. They encountered him shortly after he had clawed his way free from a Sarlacc den at the Great Pit of Carkoon. After gaining their trust and proving his loyalty, Fett was gifted a gekko to undergo his own spiritual quest and become an official member of the tribe.

Once thought to be the lethal baton of a group of savages, it is clear that the gaderffii stick carries far more importance for the Tuskens than the early settlers, intruders on the Tusken's world, could have possibly imagined. Although brandished in battle when necessary, the gaffi stick is a multifunctional accessory for defense, hunting, daily mount maintenance, and a spiritual totem. Tuskens celebrating a bountiful harvest of black melons, or other seasonal events, utilize their gaffis in ceremonial dances that symbolize the continuation of the tribe and gratitude for their place within it.

73

Moisture Vaporator

Location: Tatooine
Date: 20 BBY

Many of the settlers who make Tatooine their home rely on moisture farming and hydroponic gardening for survival and trade. In the Great Chott salt flat community alone, there are several dozen moisture farms along the southern region of the Jundland Wastes. Although these homesteads are primarily composed of interconnecting underground tunnels, marked by an entry dome, each individual lot is ringed by weather monitors, motion-detectors, and moisture vaporators.

This popular vaporator model was produced by the Pretormin Environmental Corporation. Staggered in rows like fields of crops on a more forgiving planet, each one stands about 5.6 meters (18 feet 4 inches) tall, stationed about 250 meters (273 yards) from the next, ensuring a wide berth for the optimal collection of humidity from the arid atmosphere. Microscopic droplets leached from the air are collected through the particulate filters on external condensers, then pumped into storage cisterns at the base of each spindly device. Some farms include an underground irrigation system, allowing gravity or pumps to flush the collected water through a series of pipes to the main moisture condenser at the center of the farm. A chilling unit and storage receptacle, the primary condenser is controlled by a binary processor that adjusts pH levels, filters impurities, and prepares the water for use. Homesteads typically pipe some water directly into the home for daily use, while the rest is used to maintain the health of hydroponic vegetation or for bottling to sell.

On a planet as dry as Tatooine, individual vaporators collect an average of 1.5 liters (3 pints) per day. Among the farms that have remained in operation for generations, the near-constant maintenance of aging infrastructure is costly, yet far more economic than purchasing new vaporators. Replacing an entire vaporator is expensive, with steep price hikes when trade routes are disrupted and supplies become scarce.

Moisture farming is a difficult way of life. However, for those who know no other path, giving up the independence generated by their private homestead is unthinkable.

74

The Darksaber

Location: Mandalore
Date: Before 1,000 BBY

Among the Jedi and the people of Mandalore, Tarre Vizsla is a towering figure who unified two factions that were once mortal enemies. Around 1,050 BBY, Vizsla became the first Mandalorian to join the Jedi Order. During his years of study, he crafted a unique lightsaber, a symbol of Mandalorian power: the Darksaber.

The Darksaber is a singular engineering feat among the weapons of the Jedi due to its beskar hilt, the same metal alloy that makes Mandalorian armor impervious to lightsaber blades. When ignited, it creates a blade of crackling black light, perhaps the result of the contradiction inherent in its design. After Tarre's passing, the saber was housed at the Jedi Temple on Coruscant. An heirloom for House Vizsla for centuries, the Darksaber was stolen by his descendants and became a symbol to unite the clans of Mandalore under one ruler.

Over the years, many have laid claim to the ancient weapon and the throne of Mandalore. During the Clone Wars, the Mandalorian Jedi's descendant, Pre Vizsla, used the Darksaber to overthrow the pacifist Mandalorian Duchess Satine Kryze. He then lost the blade in a duel with the former Sith Lord Maul, who had reinvented himself as the leader of a motley group of crime syndicates. The saber eventually found its way into the hands of Satine's sister, Bo-Katan Kryze. She attempted to unite Mandalore in the age of the Empire, before the Great Purge laid waste to the planet and sent the perilously few survivors into hiding.

During the early years of the New Republic, the Darksaber fell into the hands of Moff Gideon, an Imperial officer who continued to operate with impunity despite the fall of the regime he once served. The blade was returned to a Mandalorian through the ancient rite of combat around 9 ABY, when Din Djarin bested Gideon in a duel.

For many years, in the deserts of Mandalore, a magnificent statue of Tarre Vizsla kept watch over his people. Standing at some 93 meters (305 feet), the stoic face of the Mandalorian warrior, eyes downcast as if in deep thought, could be seen for miles. Those who wandered close enough, entranced by the splendor of the carving and its historical significance, saw a stone representation of the Darksaber. But Vizsla was not holding the weapon aloft as if preparing for battle. Instead, the Darksaber was ignited, the blade aimed downward, symbolically pointing to the soil of the planet the Mandalorian people called home.

75

Mythosaur Skull

Location: Nevarro
Date: 9 ABY

For centuries, the united clans of Mandalore upheld their cultural beliefs, traditions steeped in combat and a shared code of honor. Across the galaxy, they became known as a righteous but violent society, warriors who settled disputes through blood and battle. The Mandalorian people were so fearless that their leader Mandalore the Great waged a war with the Jedi Order, despite the religious sect's ability to harness the Force.

However, long before Mandalorians became established on Mandalore, legends tell of the gigantic horned sea beasts that once ruled the planet: the mythosaurs. Tales claim that these creatures coexisted with the mighty warriors, and that the Mandalorians even rode bareback upon the beasts, estimated to be more than 15 meters (50 feet) long. Some tales claim that mythosaurs were tamed, while others suggest that the creatures remained wild and free, making the Mandalorian ability to use them as mounts an even greater feat.

This beskar reproduction of a mythosaur skull can only begin to help us understand how these massive beasts lived. On either side of the face, two horns curl toward its jaw. These sharp tusks would have helped the creature battle competitors or perhaps hunt for prey. Many questions remain. Was the mythosaur a lumbering beast, moving slowly and purposefully, knowing it was the apex predator of its environment? Or was it fast and agile, nimble enough to creep up on unsuspecting prey and pounce before its victim realized what danger it was in? We may never know.

The beasts of prehistory are extinct, the only evidence of their fearsome stature left behind in fossilized bone and stories whispered to children tucked up in their beds. However, the skull of the mythosaur survives as a powerful emblem of the Mandalorian people. Images of it are worn proudly on pauldrons or displayed over doorways leading to their most sacred spaces.

First Order Era

A threat to the New Republic emerges: the paramilitary group known as the First Order. Birthed from the debris of the Empire in the Unknown Regions, the First Order kidnaps children and brainwashes them to become stormtroopers serving a shadowy Supreme Leader.

Among their ranks stands the son of Han Solo and Leia Organa. Once known by the name Ben, he falls to the darkness to become Kylo Ren, hiding his face beneath a mask not unlike his grandfather, Darth Vader. In the aftermath, Luke Skywalker vanishes into exile and Solo returns to the simpler life of a smuggler. Organa becomes the leader of the Resistance, a rebellion born out of the growing need to snuff out the First Order, while the New Republic struggles to maintain interplanetary peace.

On the world of Exegol, the Sith Eternal toils in secret, planning to restore Palpatine to his former glory and the Sith's stranglehold on the galaxy.

76

Ancient Jedi Texts

Location: Ajan Kloss
Date: c. 25,025 BBY

The small library of sacred Jedi texts is among the oldest of all the galaxy's artifacts. In the founding days of the Jedi Order, devotees relied on handwritten scripture and the ancient practice of passing knowledge from generation to generation via word of mouth. More modern Jedi recorded such intel on holocrons and datachips stored in droids, but there is an elegant simplicity to the archaic databank found within these uneti-pulp pages.

Once scattered across the stars, this collection of eight bound books and scrolls—in remarkable condition despite their age—was brought together by a man considered to be the last Jedi, Luke Skywalker. After the war that brought down the Empire, Skywalker's quest for knowledge led him to embark on an archaeological hunt for artifacts and books as he attempted to teach himself the old ways of the Jedi and bring about a new Order. At the same time he had to keep any Sith relics he found out of the hands of those who would use them to enslave and destroy.

Despite the wealth of knowledge he assembled, in the year 34 ABY, just before his death, Skywalker attempted to destroy the texts by torching the library he kept at his island home on Ahch-To. Fortunately, his final pupil, the scavenger Rey Skywalker, absconded with the unique collection before it could be consumed in the fire.

Within these volumes, myth and fact comingle as these early historians attempt to quantify their limited, but expanding, knowledge of the Force and the cosmos. Esoteric teachings on utilizing the energy binding all life to heal wounds—as detailed in the *Chronicles of Brus-bu*—and even methods of altering the course of time itself can be found alongside theorems for Padawans in training and meditation guidance. There are also examples of writing akin to poetry—although the nuance of the wordplay tends to be lost in the translation from ancient tongue to Galactic Basic. The texts do not end with

the deaths of each book's original author. The Jedi encouraged their students to update passages as they saw fit, elaborating on knowledge and sometimes solving conundrums on scraps of paper they later placed between the bound pages. In this way, the writings themselves may date back a thousand generations, yet at the same time remain almost contemporary, with some entries annotated as recently as the era of the New Republic.

The *Aionomica*, a two-volume set preserved by the Jedi master and historian Ri-Lee Howell, details early explorations of the Force, including passages thought to have been written by the original sages. The *Aionomica* was originally intended to be a single volume, but soon expanded into a second one with a double spine, suggesting that the original author twice misjudged the number of pages required to record everything they wanted to set down. Rumors of a mysterious third volume were the subject of a forgery scandal around 300 years before the fall of the Jedi Order. Indeed, the elusive tomes became a favorite subject among fraudulent antique dealers as fascination with the Jedi grew many years after the sect's dissolution. Popular interest in this belief system can be ascribed to the prevalence of children's stories and other tall tales that greatly exaggerate the abilities and exploits of the Jedi in their prime.

Far from those exciting stories of lightsaber adventures, the ancient Jedi texts sought to preserve the sacred knowledge of those most in tune with the nature of the galaxy. However, they are not without artistic merit.

The *Rammahgon* was discovered on Ossus by Luke Skywalker, who added his own annotations to the ancient scripture. The page at right contains a hand-drawn diagram of a Sith wayfinder, presumed to be Skywalker's work.

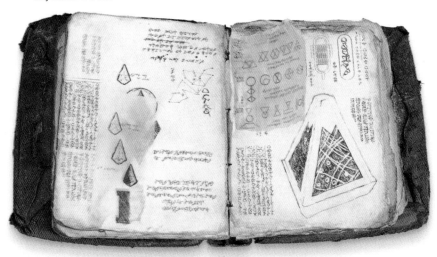

The *Rammahgon*, an influential work thought destroyed 5,000 years before the fall of the Empire, contains four origin stories of the cosmos and the Force. These conflicting accounts invite the reader to use their own experience and judgment to separate truth from fiction. Recovered from the world of Ossus, the pressed red clay cover represents an omniscient eye referenced in a poem within. But between the wordplay and talk of battling gods, there lies real, indisputable knowledge that saved the galaxy from the Sith Eternal.

On a page referencing the Sith world of Exegol, Luke Skywalker annotated his own aborted quest to find the Emperor Palpatine's wayfinder. Luke's failure, documented here, provided the information Rey needed to take up Skywalker's search. She succeeded where her master failed. By saving this small but priceless library, Rey preserved its teachings so that future students could similarly learn from—and live to rectify—the wrongs of the past.

Philosophical musings in vertical Tionese have been attributed to the Jedi Master Mott Corbet. The author of the diagram depicting the Chain Worlds Theorem remains unknown.

77

Kylo Ren's Lightsaber

Location: *Night Buzzard*
Date: 28 ABY

The lightsaber carried by Kylo Ren was a corrupted version of the weapon once crafted by his alter ego, Ben Solo. Few other objects so perfectly encapsulate the quest for balance between the Jedi and the Sith, a struggle that has shaped galactic events for millennia. Solo constructed his lightsaber while a Padawan at the Jedi school overseen by his uncle, Luke Skywalker. It had a kyber crystal that turned his blade a serene blue and a hilt that was similar to the weapon once carried by his mother, Leia Organa, during her brief Jedi training. One night at the Jedi Temple, a fateful clash between master and apprentice led to the destruction of Skywalker's academy and sent Solo fleeing into the night. Although his fall to the darkness had already begun, these events forever changed Ben Solo's destiny.

Joining forces with the Knights of Ren, Solo allowed rage and fear to consume him, reinventing himself as Kylo Ren and reforging his saber. In his fury, he split the the saber's kyber crystal down the middle. Normally, a lightsaber could not sustain such a damaged core, and the first ignition of the new blade erupted in flame, blackening the hilt's silvery sheen and damaging the inner workings. Thanks to his mechanical ingenuity—inherited from his father, Han Solo—Ren reconstructed the hilt, hardwiring a set of quillon emitters to vent the excess energy of the overclocked plasma shaft. Ren discovered that his unstable saber's explosive kyber emissions had their uses. They were ideal for stabbing opponents at close range.

The saber ironically shares attributes that date back to the era of the High Republic when the Jedi were in their prime and crossguard hilts were in fashion. Kylo Ren did not intend to pay homage to the past. The weapon's appearance was simply the necessary result of the modifications he had made.

The lightsaber of Kylo Ren thus carried the burden of Ben Solo's past in its very design. Its unstable red blade was unlike any other Jedi or Sith weapon. It existed against all odds, staying intact when it should have burned out.

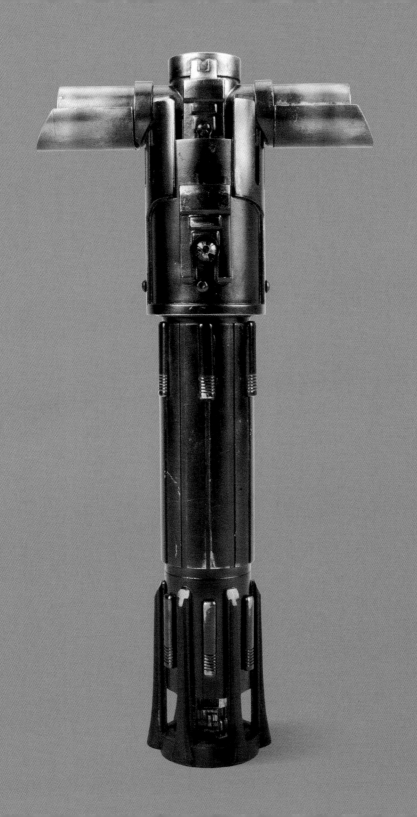

78

Lor San Tekka's Data Chip

Location: Jakku
Date: 34 ABY

Antiquated technology is easily overlooked. New discoveries quickly supplant the inventions of yesterday, and what was once cutting-edge becomes old and forgotten. That casual ignorance can create the perfect hiding place, as it did for the historian and explorer Lor San Tekka during the Resistance's desperate fight against the First Order.

San Tekka's life spanned from the end of the Republic's reign to the rise of the Resistance. He watched the Clone Wars engulf the galaxy, sadly saw the Empire rise and applauded as it fell to give birth to the New Republic. He had a deep fascination with the Jedi Order of old, and was a devotee of the Church of the Force, an underground spiritual sect that cleaved to Jedi ideals long after the Force-wielders were scattered by Order 66.

In time, Lor became close friends with the man often touted as the last of the Jedi, Luke Skywalker. When Skywalker went into self-imposed exile blaming himself for the monstrous creation of Kylo Ren, Leia Organa looked to San Tekka to study ancient data and discover Skywalker's location.

In the year 34 ABY, San Tekka succeeded in this mission. He committed a fragment of a map pointing to the first Jedi Temple to this ancient datachip. The chip was old and easily overlooked, making it the perfect hiding place. Lor kept this nondescript item secured in a leather pouch until he could pass it to Leia herself or to one of her most trusted soldiers.

San Tekka was killed by the First Order in the village of Tuanul on Jakku shortly after he discovered Skywalker's whereabouts. But before he died, he passed the data chip to Resistance pilot Poe Dameron. Combined with intel secreted in R2-D2's databanks, the knowledge San Tekka had guarded so closely ultimately led those searching for Skywalker to the far-flung world of Ahch-To—and to Skywalker himself.

79

Stormtrooper Armor

Location: Jakku
Date: 19 BBY–35 ABY

For approximately half a century, over the course of three separate but similar regimes, soldiers clad in stark, white armor stood as symbols of despotic rule. Evolving from the clone troopers of the Grand Army of the Republic, the advent of the first stormtroopers signaled the fall of democracy and the indoctrination of the galaxy by Emperor Palpatine. A similar design was adopted by the First Order paramilitary group, an offshoot of the previous regime.

Instead of conscription, luring young cadets into service with the promise of a brighter future, the First Order simply snatched children from their homes, kidnapping a new crop of soldiers who could be trained, almost from birth, to defend the leadership with their lives.

Yet the First Order's indoctrination was not entirely successful. The case of stormtrooper FN-2187 is a potent reminder of the strength of individual will. In 34 ABY, FN-2187 was deployed on his first mission in the field, headed to Jakku in a unit under the command of Captain Phasma. Searching for a datachip of personal significance to leader Kylo Ren, the troopers stormed the village of Tuanul, massacring anyone who opposed them and burning the villagers' meager homes to ash.

Caught in a crisis of conscience at the needless slaughter, FN-2187 looked on in horror as one of his squad mates was mortally wounded. As the trooper died, he smeared FN-2187's helmet with his blood.

The surviving villagers were rounded up, but when the order came to execute the last of them, FN-2187 refused to fire. His act of defiance did not go undetected and he was sent for reconditioning. This would have involved a full mental wipe—a cruel way of reprogramming erratic or willful stormtroopers—aboard Kylo Ren's flagship the *Finalizer*. Fortunately, before he could be brainwashed into mindless obedience, FN-2187 managed to escape the ship along with a Resistance spy, Poe Dameron.

The story of FN-2187—a soldier who became the Resistance general Finn—is a reminder of the heroism once attributed to stormtroopers. This general belief was cleverly exploited following the conclusion of the Clone Wars by the newly crowned Galactic Emperor Palpatine. He convinced the populace that the Jedi had turned against them and promised to create a united government and bring order to the galaxy.

Because of the respect that the majority of the people accorded them, his stormtroopers were not immediately seen as a threat to freedom, but a necessary line of defense against the fighting that had left many planets in ruins.

In those early days of the Empire, stormtroopers were presented as enforcers of the law, guardians proactively staving off further conflict.

Through conscription, the Imperial army amassed forces by promising educational incentives at the best academies. For many of the desperate and isolated youth toiling far from the Core Worlds, the Empire seemed to offer the chance to fly among the stars in pursuit of adventure.

The plastoid shell of standard-issue stormtrooper armor offered limited protection from blaster fire, but excelled in psychological warfare. When standing shoulder to shoulder, stormtroopers appeared, to the enemy, like a sea of white—one united, indistinguishable force.

Stormtroopers were sometimes mistaken for droids due to the precision of their movements. This disciplined uniformity was drummed into

The First Order stormtroopers took many aspects of their armor kits from their Imperial predecessors, including the additional shoulder pauldron that helped denote rank.

individuals during hours of grueling combat training and drills. Their helmets' visors and filtration ports formed a deliberately intimidating facade—as if frozen in an expression of grim disapproval.

Every hour spent encased in anonymizing stormtrooper armor and answering to a number instead of a name took these soldiers further and further from their own humanity. Yet beneath each helmet was an individual, just like FN-2187.

In time, cracks began to form in the Empire's prevailing narrative. Some citizens grew to despise the enforcers who coldly imposed whatever law Palpatine decreed. Imperial identification numbers—or chain codes—made even the regular denizens of the galaxy little more than nameless drones in the eyes of those in power. And the stormtroopers, scattered throughout the galaxy in various specialized units, became known for brutality masquerading as obedience.

In 5 ABY, the Empire finally fell. Toppled by a growing contingent of individuals known as the Rebel Alliance, eager for a return to true democracy. Palpatine was dethroned and his Imperial stormtroopers were left to fend for themselves, remnants of the regime. In the Empire's wake, a new paramilitary contingent —the First Order—blossomed.

Fear. Intimidation. Oppression. This was the stormtroopers' legacy. But, as the example of FN-2187 attests, their ominous armor could sometimes conceal a sympathetic human face.

At the height of the Empire's reign, from 10 to 0 BBY, stormtroopers were deployed across the galaxy in armor like this. Bulkier than the streamlined models favored by the First Order, the evolution of the design can clearly be seen in this earlier iteration.

80
Rey's Goggles

Location: Jakku
Date: 34 ABY

In the wastelands of Jakku, the Graveyard of Giants defined the landscape as an unintended monument to the finale of the Galactic Civil War. In the years after the Empire's last stand, settlers living on the desert planet mined the resources left behind during the battle. The most intrepid and adept scavengers spent years picking through the wreckage of downed Star Destroyers, including the *Ravager*, the *Inflictor*, and the *Interrogator*, searching for potentially valuable items. Among the ships' metal skeletons and the bleached bones of fallen soldiers could be found tech, components that could be cleaned and refurbished for sale or use, and also pieces of Imperial armor.

The scavenger Rey fashioned these goggles after finding a shattered stormtrooper helmet with its green-tinged lenses still intact and unmarked. Most stormtrooper helmets left to rot among the dunes became badly scoured by the sands; as a result, they contained few reusable elements. Stormtrooper helmets tended to limit the Empire's soldiers' field of vision; but by reclaiming the lenses alone, Rey was able to craft a highly effective and comfortable pair of goggles to protect her eyes from clouds of dust and sand, and the fierce glare of Jakku's sun.

The lenses are held in place by supple leather hide, most likely a scrap left over from another project, with precise hand stitching. Clips keep the goggles snugly in place over a scarf or head covering, while a fabric liner helps to absorb sweat. The lining also helps to keep the lenses from fogging up during the long hours of laborious and sometimes tedious work. On one side sits a small, salvaged light. This provided Rey with a useful, hands-free source of illumination for exploring dark places or for especially detailed work.

The goggles were just one component in a kit of tools and equipment that helped Rey survive for many years on Jakku. In 34 ABY, when she finally escaped from Niima Outpost, she left her scavenging past—along with her goggles—far behind.

81

Lanai Washstand

Location: Ahch-To
Date: 34 ABY

On an ancient island on the planet Ahch-To, coastal cliffs concealed an ancient Jedi Temple hewn from the rock. The planet's remote location in the galaxy made Temple Island a rare destination for travelers. Its native inhabitants and natural ecosystem thus remained untouched by the ravages of war, the evolution of technology, and almost the passage of time itself.

The native Lanai are a distant relation to the feathery porgs that swarm over the green hills. Unlike the curious porgs—which arrived on the island as stowaways on some visiting vessel—the Lanai created basic tools and implements for domestic tasks. They then developed the means to traverse the ocean waves that surround their home.

Male Lanais, often depicted in brightly-colored fabrics, spend much of their time at sea, returning once each lunar phase to reconnect and provide fresh food. Female Lanai remain on land, mostly keeping to the northern inlet, clad in modest white dresses and nondescript head coverings. The women tend to a number of duties to keep the island functioning and their society thriving, including the care and upkeep of the Jedi Temple.

Connected to the Force but unable to wield its power, the Lanai live in harmony with the island's abundant natural resources. This humble washstand, crafted to help keep the Lanai's clothing scrupulously clean, was probably made from driftwood or other washed-up debris. It is a point of pride with the female Lanai that their white garments should be cleaned with the same care they use to prepare their feasts and look after the island's many ancient structures.

These humble caretakers regard it as their sacred duty to maintain the Jedi Temple as part of an ancient pact between them and the Jedi peacekeepers who once sought refuge there. For thousands of years the female Lanai have journeyed from their homes in the north of the island to its southern shores to diligently preserve the Jedi huts and Temple. They go about their work daily and with quiet pride, amid the sound of the waves, the thrum of life on the island, and their own guttural singing.

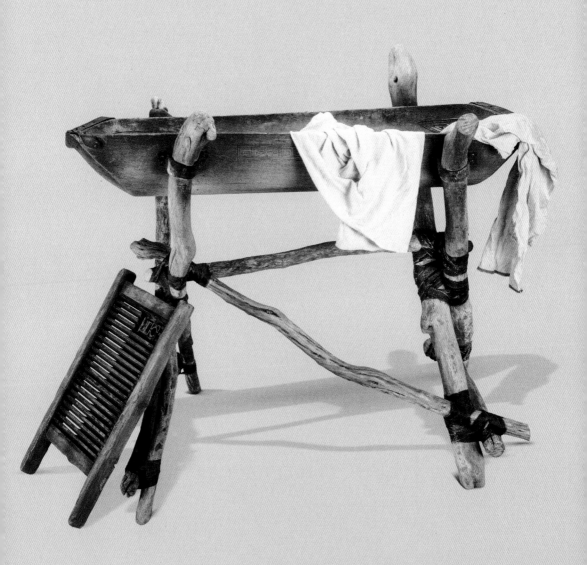

82

Electro-Shock Prod

Location: D'Qar
Date: 34 ABY

As a member of the support crew maintaining the Resistance's starfighters, an electro-shock prod was an essential part of Rose Tico's toolkit. She mainly used it for working on electrical wiring and resetting faulty systems. A dial on the device controlled the power emanating from its two prong-like electrodes. This could range from a low-powered zap to a high-voltage jolt. The small, handheld machine could restart a tripped circuit or melt an entire conduit.

Shortly after the Battle of D'Qar, Tico employed her electro-shock prod in a very different way: to reset the attitude of the freedom fighter Finn. Rose caught Finn preparing to abscond in an escape pod, on his way to warn his friend Rey against a planned rendezvous that he was sure would jeopardize both her and the rest of the fleet. Had anyone else glimpsed the Rebel hero appearing to run away in fear from the First Order, Finn's story might have ended there with a blaster bolt to the back. Tico, perhaps out of respect for Finn's past deeds on behalf of the Resistance, was merciful: she only zapped him with enough power to briefly render him unconscious.

After the First Order destroyed the Resistance base in the Otomok system, Rose joined the cause with Paige, her older sister. Paige became a gunner on one of the Resistance fleet's bombers, but bravely sacrificed her life destroying the First Order Siege Dreadnought *Fulminatrix* during the Battle of D'Qar. However, the Resistance was more than ships and machines. The real lifeblood of the cause were people like Rose Tico, who, even in her grief over her sister's sacrifice continued to believe in its ideals and dream of a better future.

Individuals like Tico—toiling in the background with her electro-shock prod and other tools, performing the vital tasks that allowed frontline heroes to shine—rarely got the recognition they deserved. A dedicated and brilliant technician who showed great courage in desperate circumstances, Rose Tico's commitment to the Resistance never wavered.

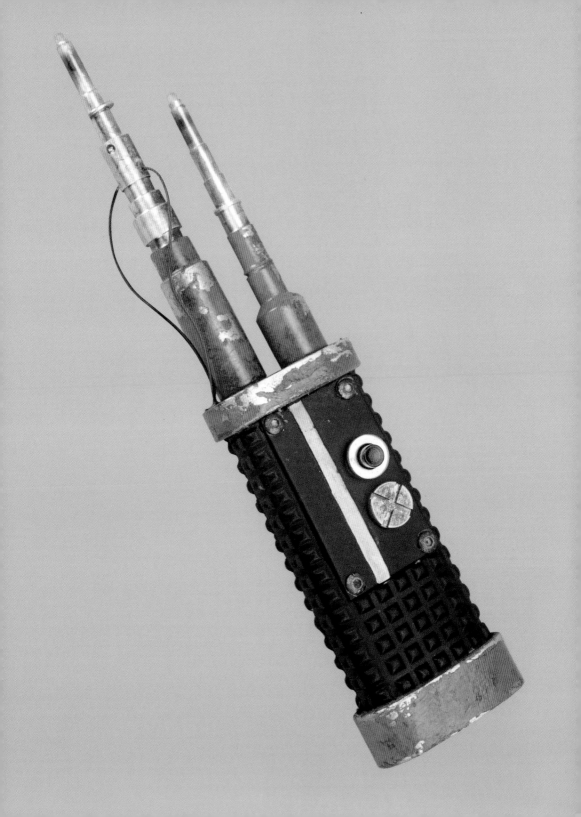

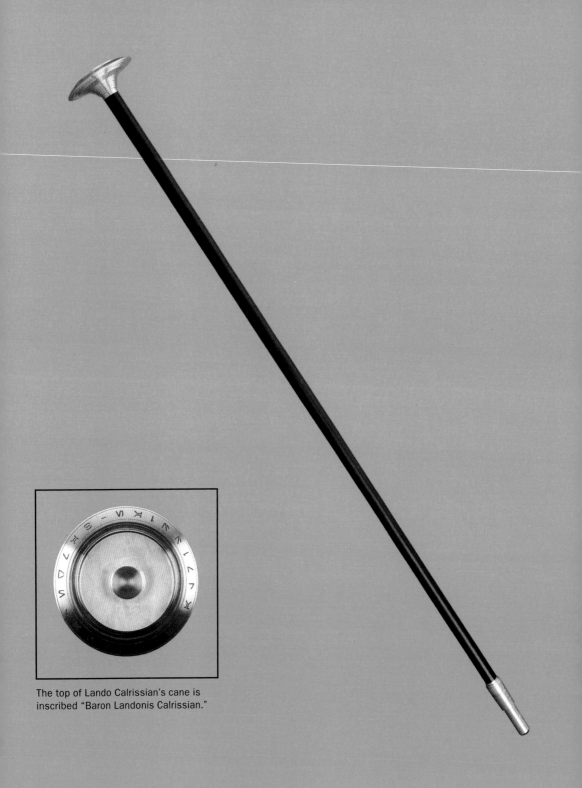

The top of Lando Calrissian's cane is inscribed "Baron Landonis Calrissian."

83

Lando's Cane

Location: Ajan Kloss
Date: 35 ABY

Lando Calrissian played many roles in his life. As a gambler in various dark dens of scum and villainy, his charismatic presence was enhanced by an array of sumptuous capes from his well-appointed closet. For a time, he parlayed a winning streak and his love of luxury into a stint as a Bespin-based businessman, acting as Baron Administrator of Cloud City's tibanna gas-mining facility. To profit from the Empire's favor, he sold out one of his oldest friends, Han Solo, in a deal with the Imperial elite. At the last moment Lando fled the floating metropolis to join the Rebellion, just as the Empire took control. His change of heart altered the course of his life and the trajectory of the galaxy. Without Lando at the helm of the *Millennium Falcon* during the Battle of Endor, the Imperial forces may well have succeeded in silencing the Rebels once and for all.

In his later years, Calrissian rejoined the Resistance at the behest of General Leia Organa. He returned to the cause from a retirement punctuated by a fruitless six-year search for his daughter Kadara, abducted by the First Order when she was just a toddler.

Lando carried this cane at the Resistance base on Ajan Kloss where, as one of the last of the old guard, he mourned Leia Organa's passing and recommitted himself to carrying on the fight. The lacquered, black cane was fashioned from greel ebonwood. It was finished with metallic caps on either end, cast from ore mined in Velser's Ring, an asteroid field in the Bespin system. Primarily intended to aid the aging general's mobility, the cane also complemented Calrissian's impeccable sense of style. The top is sculpted to resemble Cloud City itself and inscribed with the title he bore while residing there. And yet, it would be a mistake to look upon Calrissian even in those twilight years as if he were old or infirm. Anyone foolish enough to suggest such a thing might well have found themselves receiving a jab from his cane's aeroxite tip as a stern reminder of his past achievements.

84

Rey's Aki-Aki Necklace

Location: Pasaana
Date: 35 ABY

The unforgiving nature of desert worlds often makes them synonymous with struggle. Few lifeforms thrive in these desolate locations, but fortunately water collects in the shadows of the planet Pasaana's towering sandstone cliffs, allowing for the peaceful but austere existence of the native Aki-Aki.

To give thanks for these natural resources, for centuries the Aki-Aki have taken part in the Festival of the Ancestors, a colorful and joyous celebration of their culture—an explosion of music, theater, dance, and feasting that attracts some 500,000 revelers. Taking place once every 42 years, a confluence in the harvest cycle when both food and water are plentiful, the festival pays homage to the dual nature of the Aki-Aki's planet and life itself.

Visitors to the event are welcome, often greeted by handmade gifts like this husk necklace. Consisting of carefully strung beads, the pattern is interrupted by five husk dolls woven to resemble individual members of the Aki-Aki tribe in their festival garb.

The artifact speaks to the Aki-Aki's commitment not to waste any of their planet's natural resources. The yellow husks from which the necklace is made are first soaked in water to make them pliable. They are then dyed, and patiently shaped into small figures, right down to the bifurcated tusks at the bottom of what are otherwise featureless faces.

Rey's search for a Sith wayfinder took her to Pasaana while the festival was in full swing, and Aki-Aki teenager Nambi Ghima gave her the necklace. Kylo Ren's Force-bond with Rey later enabled him to steal it and track Rey down on Pasaana.

85

Military-Grade Ration Pack

Location: Jakku
Date: c. 5 ABY

The Galactic Civil War left behind many unintended monuments to the clash between the Empire and the Rebellion. On the world of Jakku, the final battle that ushered in the dawn of the New Republic was long-remembered through the so-called Graveyard of Giants, where the wreckage of war machines was looted or repurposed by desperate scavengers, such as the young Rey. Valuable mechanical components and metals were stripped out and sold or traded for food and other supplies, leaving the bones of once-magnificent Star Destroyers to rust away.

As well as metal and other useful technology, some scrappers collected Imperial rations, military-grade sustenance that had been dehydrated and compressed into easy-to-ship pouches. These synthetic, non-perishable foodstuffs even formed the basis of the local economy at Niima Outpost for a time, a junkyard settlement on Jakku under the control of the unscrupulous Crolute Unkar Plutt.

The writing on the pack is aurebesh for "portion." Dehydrated, nutrient-rich hunks of veg-meat are sealed in one half of the pouch, while the other half contains polystarch powder. Once water is added, these substances become a meal that is—if not palatable—at least enough to survive on.

At Niima Outpost, Plutt also controlled water rations. This gave him even more power over those who worked for him.

During the reign of the Empire, these ration packs were only used under special circumstances; soldiers usually traveled aboard vessels equipped with well-stocked kitchens. The packs were issued before lengthy missions or deployment to hostile environments where sustenance might be scarce.

When hydrated and gently agitated, the pack's polystarch fermented into a small bread-like roll, and the veg-meat expanded slightly, becoming less dry. Without rehydration, although the packet was safe to consume, an already distasteful experience verged on the intolerable.

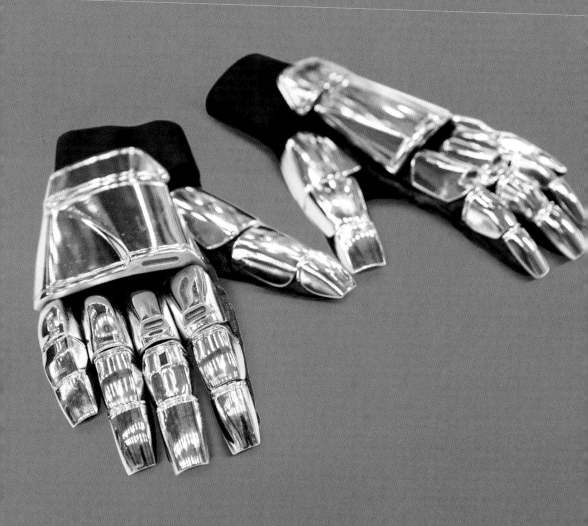

86

Captain Phasma's Crushgaunts

Location: Parnassos
Date: 34 ABY

Fanatically loyal to the First Order, Captain Phasma revered the paramilitary group's Imperial predecessor and what she considered its success in bringing order to the galaxy. Even as she ascended the ranks, she never tired of leading troops into battle. This marked her out as a rarity among First Order officers, most of whom preferred to command from a safe distance. Her harsh upbringing as a member of the Scyre clan on the nuclear wasteland of Parnassos gave Phasma a cutthroat edge. Standing 2 meters (6 feet 7 inches) tall and clad in a set of silvery fatigues, she certainly stood out from the ranks of the First Order's white-armored stormtroopers.

Phasma's distinctive outfit was not just for show—she made a number of modifications to standard-issue equipment to enhance her battlefield abilities. Her crushgaunts' reinforced armor plating protected her fingers while simultaneously magnifying her already formidable strength. Stormtrooper gloves provided basic protection for a soldier's hands. Phasma's crushgaunts enabled her to crush an enemy's bones to powder.

Salvaged Naboo chromium, said to be stripped off a yacht built for Emperor Palpatine himself, coated Phasma's armor. The chromium added an extra layer of protection to her stormtrooper gear.

A specially fabricated helmet also set her apart. It was fitted with sensors that heightened her awareness, allowing her clarity in situations that left others bewildered and confused. Frozen in an expression of menacing disapproval, her headgear's mirrored finish ensured that the last thing those who faced Phasma in combat saw before they died was their own terrified faces reflected back at them.

Despite all these impressive augmentations Captain Phasma was not invincible. In time, she would be felled by the Rebels Rose Tico and Finn—formerly First Order stormtrooper FN-2187, who had had to endure serving under her cruel leadership.

87

Resistance Ring

Location: Coruscant
Year: 1 ABY

An antique from the early days of the Galactic Civil War, this ring was worn by freedom fighters for decades, including during the conflict between the Resistance and the First Order.

At first glance, a fanlike pattern of intricate inset pieces covers the face of the ring where a stone on a higher-priced band would otherwise be set. With one deft gesture by the wearer, a small lever triggers the iris to expand. Shutters fold back into the golden circle to reveal a starbird, the symbol of the Alliance to Restore the Republic.

The silver crest design can be found across the galaxy as graffiti and on homemade trinkets carried by those fighting to restore democracy and unseat the Empire. Its appearance within this ring, once worn by Resistance mechanic Rose Tico, suggests it was originally the property of a high-ranking member of the Rebel Alliance during the early days of the Empire. Set in a gleaming aurodium-plated shell, the ring's hidden crest would have been flashed in the halls of the Imperial Senate to show support for the growing Rebel cause and assuage the fears of allies concealed within the government. In the build-up to all-out civil war, the message the ring conveyed was one of hope and fellowship.

Like the Rebel Alliance itself, the silver starbird, with its stylized wingtips and tail reaching toward the skies, was hidden. It floated in a crimson lacquered sea, as if awaiting the time the full forces of resistance could be unleashed and the Republic restored.

Rose Tico was gifted the ring following the sudden death of her heroic sister, Paige and the evacuation of the Resistance base at D'Qar. Rose later gave the emblem to a young fathier stablehand in the corrupt casino city of Canto Bight. She hoped to provide the boy with the belief that his situation, seemingly bleak, might one day improve.

88

Calligraphy Set

Location: Jedi temple, Ossus
Date: c. 28 ABY

As a young man, Ben Solo—the son of Leia Organa and Han Solo and heir to the Skywalker lineage of Force-sensitive Jedi—showed an interest in history and the arts. This calligraphy set was found in the rubble of the Jedi Temple where young Solo studied at the feet of the Jedi Master Luke Skywalker.

Skywalker had great reverence for the history of the Jedi Order and had amassed a collection of ancient texts and other relics tied directly to Jedi teachings on philosophy and the Force. He was keen to instill in his students an appreciation of the old methods the Jedi used to record their ruminations and lessons.

The set, once owned by the Jedi Obi-Wan Kenobi and used for journaling during his exile on Tatooine, was recovered by Skywalker from Kenobi's meager home after the Jedi's death. Fittingly, Skywalker gifted the set to Ben Solo, who was named after Kenobi in honor of his dedication to protecting the Skywalker twins in their youth. The young man used the same simple tools to record his own thoughts.

The set is one of the personal items Ben kept in his sleeping quarters in Skywalker's Jedi Temple on Ossus. It consists of brushes and pens, a box with hand-punched openings to hold the writing instruments for storage or travel, rolls of parchment, and a small pen stand with an inkwell.

Ben used the set to record his conflicted and delicate emotional state. As a child of the Skywalker dynasty, he struggled more than most adolescents to balance his personal desires with the expectations of his family.

In time, the weight of those expectations, his own insecurities, and his lust for power led to him being consumed by the dark side and the persona of Kylo Ren. This calligraphy set is thus a reminder that Ben was once an innocent Padawan with few other aspirations beyond becoming a Jedi Knight.

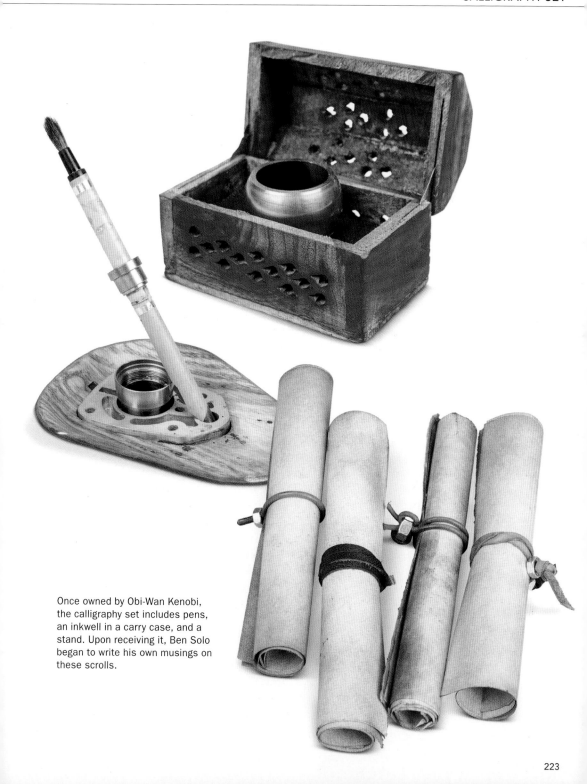

Once owned by Obi-Wan Kenobi, the calligraphy set includes pens, an inkwell in a carry case, and a stand. Upon receiving it, Ben Solo began to write his own musings on these scrolls.

89

Snoke's Slippers

Location: Exegol
Date: In use until 34 ABY

The First Order is not often equated with finery and wealth, however its figurehead had a certain flair for style. When this paramilitary group surfaced as a threat to the New Republic, it was led by the shadowy figure of Supreme Leader Snoke, who ruled while wearing these golden slippers.

A distant and cruel master, Snoke was a student of the Force who commanded his soldiers via carefully selected avatars. Meanwhile, he remained fixated on matters of the Force aboard his flagship, *Supremacy*. Snoke rarely appeared in public, and when duty necessitated it, he projected his image larger-than-life via holo message. The effect of this was to emphasize his formidable stature as an adversary and military commander.

The reality, however, was that Snoke was physically infirm owing to the cloning experimentation that had created his body. To both augment his status and protect his withering flesh, Snoke favored corded auropyle fabric khalat robes in shimmering gold with matching footwear. He decided against obscuring his malformed face, believing that his frightening appearance could be used to advantage.

Snoke wore these golden embroidered slippers, in part, to ease his perpetually aching feet. They contain extra padding to cushion each painful step. Their crimson lining matched the red armor of his Elite Praetorian Guard, eight human warriors who stood ready to defend his throne. He was wearing this pair when he met his demise in the year 34 ABY, cleaved in two by the Skywalker saber after fatally miscalculating his pupil Kylo Ren's true intentions.

Snoke's slippers are a reminder of the First Order's obsession with the past, when royal houses clothed themselves in finery while their subjects struggled to obtain the basic necessities of life. Ultimately, Snoke was just a Sith puppet, a servant to the cause whose sole purpose was to groom young Ben Solo to become an agent of evil like his late grandfather, Darth Vader.

90

Fathier Racing Saddle

Location: Cantonica
Date: 34 ABY

Fathier racing is a popular sport among the extravagantly wealthy who frequent the racetracks of the casino city of Canto Bight on Cantonica. They bet exorbitant amounts on their favorite fathier, based on their belief in the prowess of a particular rider, a hot tip from a stable, or simply because they like the sound of an animal's racing name.

Fathiers were brought to Canto Bight from a Republic member world. Most are more than 3 meters (10 feet) high at the shoulder with long ears, soulful eyes, and short coats of bristly hair. Beneath the glittering city of Canto Bight, these noble creatures spend their days in stalls barely large enough for their muscular bodies. Tended to by slaves, often children, who are forced to sleep in the same stalls, the creatures bray to one another from behind locked doors. Their mournful song reflects their mutual loyalty, which is also evident in the family-like hierarchy of wild fathier herds.

Fathiers can gallop at speeds of up to 75 kph (47 mph). On the track, riders use saddles to stay on board. Built with only the comfort of the jockey in mind, these heavily padded seats enable a rider to spend hours training their fathier at a grueling clip. This saddle's girth includes several hand-punched notches, indicating that the rider needed to tighten it as the animal grew thinner. Fathiers often become emaciated due to malnourishment or from drugs that are employed to push their bodies to unnatural speeds.

Those fathiers which prosper on the circuit and make their benefactors wealthy usually enjoy a reasonably comfortable life, with proper nourishment and care. A few retire to experience relative freedom, living out their days grazing grassy meadows. However, if a fathier is injured, deemed too slow, or becomes too old to race, it is likely to suffer a cruel fate. The leather used to make a saddle such as this was probably skinned from fathiers who were no longer of any use to their owners.

91

Homing Beacon Bracelet

Location: D'Qar
Date: 34 ABY

Homing beacon technology has been utilized by bounty hunters and law-enforcement agencies for decades. In more recent times, this sophisticated technology has become even more compact, allowing beacons to be secreted in individuals' clothing or surreptitiously worn as statement jewelry.

Even before agreeing to become her Master in Jedi training, Leia Organa shared an immediate connection with Force-sensitive freedom fighter Rey Skywalker. The two women were aligned in purpose and linked by more than blood: Rey formed a rare dyad in the Force with Leia's son, Ben Solo. Leia and Rey were also bound together by circumstance. Having lost her entire world and her family because of the actions of the Sith-controlled Empire, Leia empathized with the orphaned young scavenger from Jakku.

Before Rey departed for Ahch-To on a desperate mission to bring Luke Skywalker back into the Resistance fold, Leia gave her an S-thread transmitter beacon bracelet "to light her way home," as she put it. It was twinned with this beacon, which Leia wore on her wrist. Despite Rey's courageous dedication to the Rebel cause, Leia sensed that the young woman's history of abandonment might make it especially difficult for her to venture to the faraway Jedi Temple on Ahch-To without a link to remind her of her found family among the Resistance fighters. And for Leia—having lost one child to the conflict already—the glow of the beacon on her wrist was a source of comfort, tangible proof of their connection.

Kept hidden among the jewels and baubles that she customarily wore to respect her royal pedigree and her mother Breha's teachings, the homing beacon linked Leia to Rey across thousands of light years. Its little glowing orb reinforced a promise Leia had made herself: never to lose another child to the darkness.

92

C-3PO's Red Arm

Location: Taul
Date: 33 ABY

The golden protocol droid C-3PO served the Royal House of Organa for many decades. He was first employed in the palace on Alderaan and then among the royal command fleet serving Senator Bail Organa. For years C-3PO faithfully stood at the elbow of Organa's daughter, Princess Leia.

At the time of the New Republic, C-3PO worked as the senator's personal attaché in delicate matters that required the droid's exceptional linguistic abilities. His circuits housed more than 7 million forms of communication, but the droid was notably less adept at understanding the nuances of human emotion. However, after witnessing years of torment and strife, from the harsh sands of Tatooine where he was built to the frontlines of no less than three galaxy-encompassing wars, C-3PO retained a keen understanding of personal sacrifice.

Any droid in service long enough will see their various internal and external parts and pieces replaced and renewed. But this particular red limb, worn by C-3PO as war with the First Order was breaking out, was a reminder of another droid's destruction and sacrifice—later mirrored by C-3PO's own submission to a memory wipe in service to the Resistance cause.

On the world of Taul, C-3PO and several other droids were victims of a crash landing that forced them to traverse this dangerous, swamp-ridden world while awaiting rescue. Among their ranks was a crimson-plated prisoner, 0-MR1 ("Omri"), a First Order droid who held the key to retrieving Resistance Admiral Gial Ackbar from captivity behind enemy lines. During their ordeal, Omri gave up the valuable intel and sacrificed himself to allow C-3PO's continued survival. While the rest of the droid's mechanical parts were destroyed by an acid rainstorm, C-3PO was able to retrieve an arm, which was later used to replace his own lost left limb. Except for its coloration, it was an exact match.

C-3PO kept the arm while based at the Resistance hub on D'Qar. As the only physical remnant of Omri, a foe who turned into a friend, it is a reminder that all sentient forms, be they organic or machine, are capable of great acts of bravery.

93

The Mask of Darth Vader

Location: Coruscant
Date: 34 ABY

From the ashes of the Republic, the Empire rose to power, reshaping the galaxy in the aftermath of the Clone Wars. No single object better encompasses those dark times than the helmet worn by Emperor Palpatine's right hand, the Sith Lord and Imperial enforcer Darth Vader.

The reemergence of this object in the era of the First Order—more than two decades after Vader's demise—cast the man who wore it in the role of hero in the eyes of Kylo Ren, a high-ranking official in the paramilitary group, who was also Vader's grandson. The mask came to be a highly prized item in Ren's collection of historical artifacts. It may have been salvaged on the Forest Moon of Endor from Vader's funeral pyre, a sacred burial rite for flesh, bone, and the suit that sustained him for the wretched second half of his life.

Whether damaged by fire or in a pristine state as part of Vader's life-preserving suit, the mask retains a haunting, skull-like quality. It is both a warning for those tempted by the darkness and a threat to those walking in the light.

The obsidian helmet was a medical marvel at the time it was forged. It represented a complex advance in science and technology only made possible by the demands of the war and the needs of clone soldiers serving on the front lines. Many clones who were injured in the line of duty could be rebuilt to continue the crusade.

After the Jedi Anakin Skywalker was mortally wounded in a lightsaber duel with Obi-Wan Kenobi on Mustafar, he was outfitted with the mask by droids in the Grand Republic Medical Facility on Coruscant. The life-saving surgery transformed him into the fearsome Darth Vader. This alter ego was such a drastic shift, both in appearance and temperament, that some observers believed that the Sith Lord Vader had murdered Skywalker, instead of recognizing the monster he had truly become.

This view of Vader's helmet from when he was alive exudes power and menace.

Vader was given cybernetic enhancements simply to function anything like normally. His was a miserable, pain-ridden existence, made slightly more bearable thanks to a protective exoskeleton that protected his fragile body. The helmet worked in conjunction with a life-preserving suit of durasteel and synthetic fibers.

Magnetically locking into place, the helmet helped Vader to breathe via a ventilation system. This enabled him to take a wheezing intake and exhalation of breath as filtered air reached his sensitive lungs and regulated his body temperature.

A gaiter at the base of the helmet supported Vader's neck and contained a nutrient feeding tube. Red-tinted lenses compensated for the weakened vision of his organic eyes, calibrated colors, and enhanced his field of view. A frilled armored helmet interlocked with the mask to form an airtight seal. This created a meticulously maintained environment inside the armor, which thus became both a shield from the external world and a prison for the tormented soul within.

Beyond its clinical functionality, the mask became a potent symbol of the tyrannical Imperial regime. Vader was known to employ the Force to make captives talk, but frequently the mere sight of Vader's helmeted, black-clad figure was enough to compel testimony from those he wished to question.

With its striking design, it was impossible to know what emotion might be playing across the face of what was left of the man beneath.

The mask of Darth Vader became synonymous with everything the Empire became: faceless, imposing, and cruel. And beneath the helmet lay an equally powerful symbol of the ruins of the Republic, a man who had been lauded as the greatest of the Jedi Order, the Chosen One of prophecy, destined to bring balance to the Force. At the time the helmet was created, Anakin Skywalker and the Republic were no more, symbols of a past grandeur soon to be reduced to shadow and myth.

These images reveal some of the inner workings of the helmet and neck brace.

94

Poe Dameron's Flying Jacket

Location: D'Qar
Date: c. 34 ABY

This style of rugged leather flying jacket was popular among Resistance pilots. It was tough enough to withstand heavy wear and it was also flame retardant. Unlike the orange flight suits also utilized among starfighters units, this brown-and-red jacket could easily blend in amid a crowd, making it the preferred attire for secret military operations and rebel spies.

The condition of the jacket speaks to the scrappy spirit of the Resistance and its core values of fellowship and sustainability. Due to waning resources, the Resistance leadership was known to reuse everything from apparel to junked ships, patching together gear and fighter craft from whatever parts and pieces they could obtain. In contrast to the polished sheen of the First Order's stormtroopers and their immaculately uniformed officers, Resistance fighters often appeared scruffy and battle-scarred. First Order propaganda had no difficulty painting the comparatively unkempt Rebel forces as terrorists and threats to peace and order. However, the Rebels' individualistic attitudes served them well. They reflected their mindset that hope could still flourish despite seemingly overwhelming odds.

This garment originally belonged to Poe Dameron, a New Republic Navy defector often regarded as the best pilot among the Resistance. He was wearing it when trying to escape from the First Order in a TIE fighter along with a defecting stormtrooper known as FN-2187.

When their spacecraft was shot down and crashed, FN-2187, soon to be renamed Finn, salvaged the jacket. Convinced his new comrade Poe was dead, Finn shrugged off the stormtrooper armor that had defined his life up to that point and proudly donned the jacket. A crucial part of his new Rebel identity, the garment seemed an emblem of hope. Later, when Finn was badly injured during the Battle of Starkiller Base, Poe repaired its tatters and tears. As a definitive gesture of friendship, he returned the jacket to Finn.

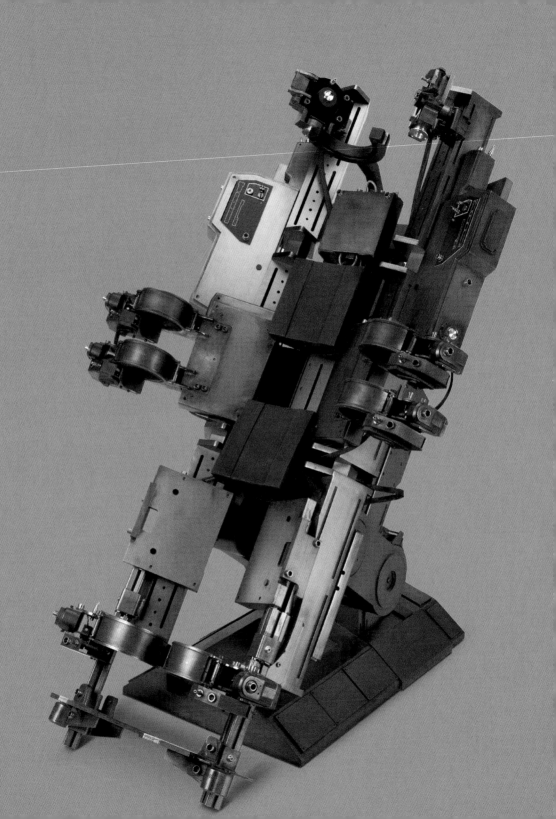

95

Interrogation Chair

Location: *Finalizer*
Date: 34 ABY

The First Order's DNA, from its aspirations to its armor, sprang from the remnants of the Empire. So, too, did its penchant for compelling cooperation from its enemies. The basic design of interrogation chairs remained largely unchanged for decades. An offshoot of equipment found in the operating suites of Galactic Republic medical facilities, the chairs kept captives prone, tilted at an angle to accentuate physical discomfort. Manacles immobilized the prisoner, while an array of electrified probes, cutting tools, syringes, and other implements were hidden just out of sight. Both the manacles and the assortment of interrogation tools could be easily customized.

According to the logs of several officers, the First Order chair was an improvement on Imperial models. In those days, interrogator droids were deployed to extract information. While they were still used by some in the First Order, the droids could not compare to a fully equipped torture suite. After all, what is more terrifying for a captive than the unknown? Without warning, a prisoner could be incapacitated by a sharp jolt of electricity, rendering them numb, speechless, or even unconscious. Some enforcers preferred to begin with cutting tools—small, spherical blades that buzzed into life and appeared seemingly out of nowhere. Sometimes interrogators didn't even question their captives. They wore them down until victims were eager to volunteer any information that might grant them a moment free from pain.

Before his ascent to Supreme Leader, Kylo Ren reveled in crushing his enemies in all manner of ways, but torture was among his favorites—an outlet for the seething rage penned up inside him. During his pursuit of his former Jedi Master, Luke Skywalker, he used an interrogation chair on both Poe Dameron and the Force-sensitive scavenger Rey. In addition to the standard tools, Ren was not above using the Force to reach into the minds of his prisoners and extract information, a tactic used as a last resort when all else had failed to induce cooperation.

96

Kylo Ren's Helmet

Location: Exegol
Date: 35 ABY

Kylo Ren was a creation of Ben Solo's own choosing, although Solo alone was not solely to blame for the rise of his dark alter ago. Ren was born out of a toxic mix of loneliness, Skywalker blood, seething resentment, and expertly manipulated fear. In this way, Ren took over the personality of Han Solo and Leia Organa's only son. Ren relinquished his claim to the Skywalker dynasty and the path of the Jedi. He stepped into the shadow of his grandfather, Darth Vader, and devoted himself to the dark side.

To complete his transformation, in the year 28 ABY, Ren forged a helmet in the style of the battle armor of the Knights of Ren he commanded. It paid homage to Vader's life-saving black mask. At the front, silvery inlay accentuated the visor, concealing Ren's eyes and emotions. A triangular mouthpiece, controlled by servomotors, covered his mouth. It contained a built-in vocoder that dramatically lowered the pitch of his voice. On the rare occasions Ren wished to show his face, releasing the mouthpiece allowed him to remove the snug-fitting helmet.

Kylo Ren was a complex, conflicted young man. He desperately wished to leave his past behind and forcibly cut himself off from his family—and the light—by murdering his own father. Yet, when he gazed upon the mask of Darth Vader—kept for several years in his private collection—did Ren truly believe that he was continuing Vader's legacy by his actions? Vader, after all, had been redeemed at the end of his life by the very man, Luke Skywalker, whom Ren claimed to hate above all others.

Kylo Ren's mask was intended to intimidate his enemies, but Ren's dark side master, Snoke, mocked him for wearing it, seeing it as an affectation. Vader's helmet was a means of serving out a life sentence of anguish. Ren's helmet served only to give Ben Solo a way to hide his face and frighten underlings. In Snoke's estimation, Ben needed his helmet to pretend he was someone else, mask his conflicted heart, and conceal his identity. By contrast, without his helmet, Vader could simply not have survived. Snoke was known to berate his pupil as "a child in a mask" and Ren smashed his helmet in a fit of rage after a particularly harsh dressing down. Anger fueled Ren's own rebellion. He murdered Snoke on his throne and took his place as the Supreme Leader of the First Order.

In 35 ABY, the helmet was reforged by a Symeong metalworker named Albrekh. Instead of commissioning a completely new helmet, Ren chose to have the pieces of his broken one remade at a Sith forge. Albrekh's painstaking work joined the shards together with Sarrassian iron.

The final form of Kylo Ren's mask was much stronger than the original. It was also a more fitting facade. Instead of hiding Ren's true nature, it reflected the trauma and inner conflicts he had endured. The reforged helmet suggested a web of scar tissue or a network of veins. It symbolized the strength of his bloodline and the power of his shattered soul, pieced back together by Sith ingenuity.

Although he did not require the helmet to instill fear in his followers, he found that he greatly enjoyed the way it made them cower. His helmet helped to cement his place among the Knights of Ren. He felt he really belonged.

Without Snoke's scorn holding him back, Ren focused his attention on the ancient ways of the Sith. He found a pathway to Exegol—the hidden planet of the Sith occultists—and attacked what remained of the Resistance. However, to some who served under the Supreme Leader, Ren's new helmet was the totem of a deeply troubled man. Few spoke out against Ren, given his proclivity for sudden violence, but there were those who saw his reforged helmet as the sign of a deeply insecure leader.

Wearing his splintered past as a badge of honor effectively exposed and paraded his internal conflicts for all to see. To those who knew his story, Kylo Ren became both a leader to fear and someone to be pitied.

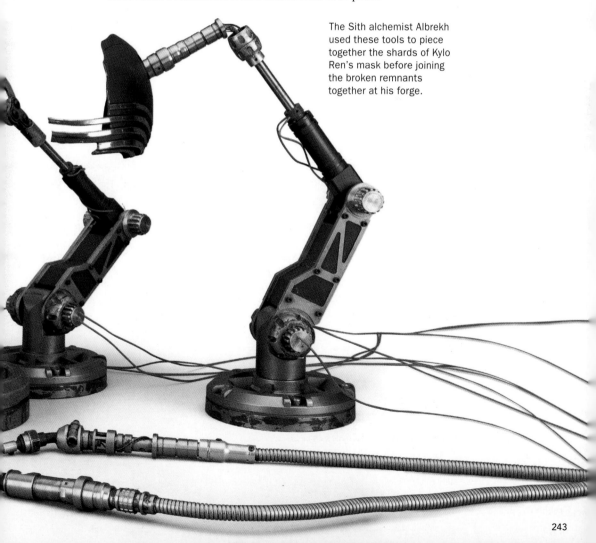

The Sith alchemist Albrekh used these tools to piece together the shards of Kylo Ren's mask before joining the broken remnants together at his forge.

97

Sith Wayfinder

Location: Kef Bir
Date: 35 ABY

For thousands of years, dating back to the earliest interstellar travel, the Jedi and the Sith used wayfinders to chart a course among the stars. A technological precursor to modern navicomputers, wayfinders were essential for early hyperspace exploration.

Today, wayfinders are exceptionally rare. Modern engineers and scientists have put little effort into studying the few known specimens, dismissing them as sorcery. As a result, the mechanism that allows a wayfinder to plot a course through the Unknown Regions remains a mystery. Reinforced with a frame of hardened Kathol resin, this wayfinder has a supraluminite lodestone core trapped in plasmatic energy—presumably harvested from nebular space— encased in Cybotaro waxen glass etched with star charts.

Emperor Palpatine was fascinated by ancient treasures and maintained a vault of relics from the Jedi and the Sith on the world of Pillio. However, he kept his most valuable artifacts close at hand, including one of two wayfinders capable of pointing the way to the Sith world of Exegol.

According to legend, the Sith Lord Darth Noctyss was similarly obsessed with the pursuit of Force knowledge and the secrets of lost civilizations, in particular the quest for immortality. As her natural life span drew to an end, her search took her to Exegol. There she achieved the ability to evade death, yet paid a terrible price, being transformed into a pitiable, deformed creature. She was neither the first nor the last of the Sith to dedicate their lives to the darkness and lose themselves in the process.

In the last years of the Empire, Darth Vader was entrusted with this Sith wayfinder to lead him to Exegol in service to his master, Darth Sidious. Kept in a safe on Mustafar after his demise, this key to passing through the veil of the Galactic Barrier was stolen by Vader's grandson, Kylo Ren, in the final days of the First Order. This act would ultimately lead the Resistance into combat with the hidden army of the Final Order. For, without the Wayfinder's coordinates, the Rebel fleet would have had no way of navigating the Western Reaches to locate Exegol and bring an offensive strike to Palpatine's door.

98

Ochi's Dagger

Location: Pasaana
Date: Unknown

Inscribed in Ur-Kittât, the runic language of the Sith—an ancient tongue forbidden since the days of the Old Republic—this ornate dagger was a ceremonial object in service to the dark side. The dagger was formerly owned by the Sith occultist and assassin Ochi of Bestoon. It was forged in a manner that seems to vibrate through the Force itself, bestowing a personality of sorts upon the weapon.

Those that have encountered the dagger and lived to tell the tale speak of an insatiable bloodlust that seems to emanate from the blade. Those with sensitivity to the Force could touch the weapon and glimpse its dark deeds. This tragic catalog of death includes the parents of Rey Skywalker, Dathan and Miramir, murdered by Ochi around the year 21 ABY. Those who dared to grab hold of the leather-wrapped handle maintained that the blade would speak to anyone willing to listen. Storytellers of old claimed that as it sliced through flesh, the blade would become hot to the touch, as if drinking the blood of its victim. Whoever wielded the blade could commune with the dagger as if joined with its spirit. It was almost as if the being who held the weapon was at the mercy of its whims.

A full translation of the inscription on the weapon is forbidden, but it concludes with a key phrase: "Only this blade tells." In the knife's crossguard nestles a measurement arc that provided a way of pinpointing Palpatine's most treasured artifacts more than three decades after wreckage from his second Death Star landed on Kef Bir, the Ocean Moon of the Endor system. In 35 ABY, Rey used the dagger to gain access to Palpatine's Imperial Vault.

The Sith Eternal are no more, but the dagger remains, a reminder of their quest for total domination. But venture close to the blade and you can almost sense that it is longing to return to its old, evil ways. A thrum seems to emanate from it that evokes blood-curdling incantations and beckons a new master to call the weapon into service. Even those who scoff at the arcane ways of the dark side would be wise to keep their distance from this relic of a perilous bygone era.

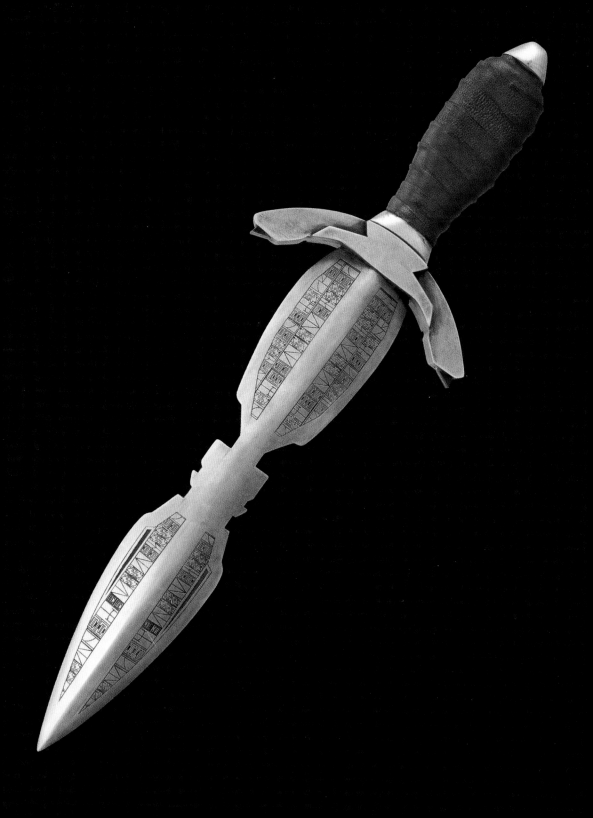

99

MDS-440 Datapad

Location: Ajan Kloss
Date: 35 ABY

Datapads are a ubiquitous form of portable technology. They enable shopkeepers to maintain inventories, bounty hunters to study their next target, and diplomats to parse complex trade agreements. Most datapads can scan and translate written languages, store personal files, receive written and auditory comms, and even tune into local communication frequencies.

The Empire provided datapads to cadets as standard-issue equipment, and high-ranking officials had their own private datapads under strict lockdown and off-network to preserve the sensitivity of certain intel. The Rebel Alliance, and later the Resistance, used the Empire's reliance on documentation to its advantage. In the hands of a Rebel, a datapad read-out could mean the difference between life and death.

This MDS-440 datapad was utilized on the star cruiser *Raddus,* formerly a New Republic ship before being recommissioned by Resistance forces. The Mon Calamari-built vessel was named for the fallen war hero who had led the Rebels' assault at the Battle of Scarif and was under the command of Gial Ackbar, a Mon Cala admiral before joining the Rebel cause.

The *Raddus* was soon destroyed in the stars above Crait in a suicide run that took down the First Order flagship *Supremacy.* Most of the *Raddus*' crew escaped in lifeboats and headed for the planet's surface. The datapad preserved the Resistance ship's essential files and shored up the freedom fighter's morale as they faced repeated First Order attacks.

The datapad's dimly lit screen still preserves file readouts from the Resistance vessel's battle-analysis computer. As the Rebels fled Crait aboard the *Millennium Falcon*, they knew that the data contained on this device could prove vital for their ability to find potential weaknesses in the enemy and mount their next attack.

100

Rey's Lightsaber

Location: Tatooine
Date: 35 BBY

Having carried the Skywalker lightsaber through the end of the war with the First Order, Rey forged her own lightsaber. Rey's hilt is more rugged than that built by Anakin Skywalker during the Clone Wars and later wielded by his son, Luke, or the elegant, rose-gold weapon once carried by Luke's sister, Leia Organa. This lightsaber is a reflection of Rey's own individual journey, the weapon of a survivor and a Jedi.

Born of the Palpatine dynasty, Rey was the biological daughter of Dathan, a Palpatine produced through genetic experimentation. Her mother Miramir was a humble junk trader on the harsh world of Jakku. Rey's Force-sensitivity made her a target, and at the age of six she was left in the care of the junk boss Unkar Plutt. Through luck and ingenuity, Rey survived in secret as a scavenger there for 13 years. Her dormant proclivity to the Force was then awakened through a chance encounter with the Skywalker saber.

After studying the mistakes of the past with Master Luke and training her body and mind on Ajan Kloss with Master Leia, Rey was instrumental in helping the Resistance defeat Palpatine and his Final Order at the Battle of Exegol.

After this victory, Rey completed her own lightsaber. The handle borrowed parts from a salvaged quarterstaff that had been Rey's weapon of choice during her years on Jakku. A comfortable grip was fashioned from the cloth that once protected her from the blistering suns and rough sands of that world. It was wrapped around the base of the weapon where the all-important kyber crystal was carefully placed. Instead of a standard switch, Rey incorporated a rotating gear to ignite the blade, which burned with a golden-yellow light indicative of the bright future ahead.

Rey also took the name Skywalker. It was the final step toward rejecting her Palpatine lineage, and honoring the sacrifices that the Skywalker clan had made to bring peace to the galaxy. A guardian worthy of her place as the last of the Jedi, she carries this weapon still.

Index

SENIOR EDITOR Alastair Dougall
PROJECT ART EDITOR Jon Hall
PRODUCTION EDITOR Marc Staples
SENIOR PRODUCTION CONTROLLER Mary Slater
MANAGING EDITOR Emma Grange
MANAGING ART EDITOR Vicky Short
PUBLISHING DIRECTOR Mark Searle

FOR LUCASFILM
EDITOR Jennifer Pooley
SENIOR EDITOR Brett Rector
CREATIVE DIRECTOR Michael Siglain
ART DIRECTOR Troy Alders
STORY GROUP Leland Chee, Pablo Hidalgo, and Kate Izquierdo
CREATIVE ART MANAGER Phil Szostak
ASSET MANAGEMENT Jackey Cabrera, Elinor De La Torre,
Bryce Pinkos, and Sarah Williams

First published in Great Britain in 2023 by
Dorling Kindersley Limited
One Embassy Gardens, 8 Viaduct Gardens,
London SW11 7BW
A Penguin Random House Company

10 9 8 7 6 5 4 3 2 1
001–332600–April/2023

Page design copyright © 2023 Dorling Kindersley Limited

© & TM 2023 Lucasfilm LTD.

The authorised representative in the EEA is Dorling Kindersley
Verlag GmbH. Arnulfstr. 124, 80636 Munich, Germany.

A CIP catalogue record for this book
is available from the British Library.
ISBN 978-0-2415-8021-9

Printed and bound in China

For the curious

www.dk.com
www.starwars.com

ACKNOWLEDGEMENTS

Dorling Kindersley would like to thank Chelsea Alon at Disney;
Kristin Baver, Jennifer Pooley, Brett Rector, Michael Siglain,
and Troy Alders at Lucasfilm; Megan Douglass for proofreading;
Julia March for the index.

Kristin Baver would like to thank Laela French, Director of
Archives for The Lucas Museum of Narrative Art, for opening
the doors at Skywalker Ranch illuminating the possibilities
suggested by all the treasures within; the Lucasfilm archivists
past and present, but especially Madlyn Moskowitz, who first
invited her to take a closer look at Lucasfilm's artifacts, and
Portia Fontes and Kari Yovetich, who keep sharing their
precious finds (even though she sometimes ask to touch them);
for Pablo Hidalgo and Jason Fry, masters of lore; this book's
fearless editor Alastair Dougall and intrepid designer Jon Hall;
Lucasfilm Publishing's Jennifer Pooley, Michael Siglain, and
Brett Rector, and everyone at Lucasfilm's Story Group, but
especially Phil Szostak and Leland Chee.

This book was made with Forest
Stewardship Council™ certified
paper - one small step in DK's
commitment to a sustainable future.
For more information go to
www.dk.com/our-green-pledge

ABOUT THE AUTHOR

Kristin Baver is the Associate Editor of StarWars.com, covering
Star Wars news, writing interview features on George Lucas and
other important figures in the *Star Wars* galaxy, as well as
spotlighting the dedicated fan community and their impressive
and imaginative creations. The author of *The Art of Star Wars:
The High Republic*, *Star Wars: Skywalker—A Family at War*, and
a contributor to *Star Wars Year by Year* as well as *Star Wars:
Timelines*, Kristin is the host of *This Week! in Star Wars*.
She previously worked as an award-winning journalist covering
crime and social issues in central Pennsylvania, but now lives
with her partner, Mike Lester, and their cat, Hector Smidget,
in San Francisco, California.